QUICK FROM SCRATCH

CHICKEN
AND OTHER BIRDS

Arroz con Pollo, page 143

QUICK FROM SCRATCH

CHICKEN
AND OTHER BIRDS

Food & Wine
BOOKS

American Express Publishing Corporation
New York

Editor in Chief: Judith Hill
Assistant Editors: Susan Lantzius and Laura Byrne Russell
Managing Editor: Terri Mauro
Copy Editor: Barbara A. Mateer
Wine Editor: Richard Marmet
Art Director: Nina Scerbo
Art Assistant: Leslie Andersen
Photographer: Melanie Acevedo
Food Stylist: Roscoe Betsill
Prop Stylist: Denise Canter
Production Manager: Stuart Handelman

Senior Vice President/Chief Marketing Officer: Mark V. Stanich
Vice President, Books and Products: Marshall A. Corey
Marketing Manager: Bruce Spanier
Senior Fulfillment Manager: Phil Black
Business Manager: Doreen Camardi
Marketing Coordinator: Richard Nogueira

Cover Design: Perri DeFino
Recipe Pictured on Front Cover: Spiced Chicken Legs with Apricots and Raisins, page 115
Page 6: *Kitchen photo,* Bill Bettencourt; *Portraits,* Chris Dinerman

AMERICAN EXPRESS PUBLISHING CORPORATION

LIBRARY OF CONGRESS CATALOGING-IN-PUBLICATION DATA AVAILABLE

ISBN 0-916103-89-7

Published by American Express Publishing Corporation
1120 Avenue of the Americas, New York, NY 10036

Printed in China.

CONTENTS

RECIPES PICTURED AEOVE: *(left to right)* pages 1⁵5, ●1, 15⁵

Perfecting a chicken dish in the FOOD & WINE Books test kitchen

Susan Lantzius trained at La Varenne École de Cuisine in Paris, worked as a chef in Portugal for a year, and then headed to New York City. There she made her mark first as head decorator at the well-known Sant Ambroeus pastry shop and next as a pastry chef, working at such top restaurants as San Domenico and Maxim's. In 1993, she turned her talents to recipe development and editorial work for FOOD & WINE Books.

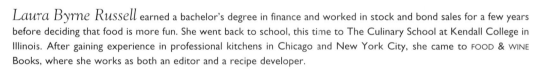

Judith Hill is the editor in chief of FOOD & WINE Books, a division of American Express Publishing. Previously she was editor in chief of COOK'S Magazine, director of publications for La Varenne École de Cuisine in Paris, from which she earned a Grand Diplôme, and an English instructor for the University of Maryland International Division in Germany. Her book credits include editing cookbooks for Fredy Girardet, Jane Grigson, Michel Guérard, and Anne Willan.

Laura Byrne Russell earned a bachelor's degree in finance and worked in stock and bond sales for a few years before deciding that food is more fun. She went back to school, this time to The Culinary School at Kendall College in Illinois. After gaining experience in professional kitchens in Chicago and New York City, she came to FOOD & WINE Books, where she works as both an editor and a recipe developer.

INTRODUCTION

The amenable chicken keeps company equally well with subtle or strong ingredients; it takes on any accent—be it Tuscan, Provençal, Mexican, or Thai—with effortless facility; and it changes character from plain to posh with ease. Because of its amazing adaptability, chicken has inspired cooks the world over, including, of course, those in the FOOD & WINE Books test kitchen. Susan Lantzius and Laura Russell, our editor/cooks, have perfected Rustic Garlic Chicken (page 117), Chicken Provençal (page 35), Chicken Burritos with Black-Bean Salsa and Pepper Jack (page 163), and Chicken Pad Thai (page 133), as well as dishes influenced by a myriad of other regions, and some purely inventive combinations.

As we conceived, developed, tested, and tasted the recipes in this book, whether we were making simple Spicy Chicken Chili (page 105) or mellow, sophisticated Sautéed Chicken Breasts with Tarragon Cream Sauce (page 25), we kept repeating, "This is too easy. Chicken goes with everything." Susan and I, with our classic French training, consider chicken the veal of today, excellent just sautéed with a sprinkling of salt, pepper, and herbs to bring out its own taste and also ideal as a background for easy sauces with complex or bold flavorings. Laura dubbed the hardworking bird *cooperative chicken*. We hope that you'll find the name apt as you try the imaginative ideas here and that you'll never again think of chicken as boring.

Very nearly as flexible and available as chicken are turkey and Cornish hens. So we considered them appropriate for a book dedicated to quick yet delectable fare for busy weeknights (though many of our recipes double as lifesavers for weekend entertaining). Hence, you'll find the likes of Turkey Breast with Mustard Sage Crumbs (page 59), Turkey with Walnut Parmesan Sauce (page 47), Cornish Hens with Fruit, Walnuts, and Honey Apple Glaze (page 85), and Grilled Cornish Hens with Sun-Dried-Tomato Pesto (page 93).

We developed each of these recipes with the thought that it should be a solid main dish, needing, if anything, only the addition of a totally no-fuss accompaniment, such as a salad or bread. We included other just-as-fast menu suggestions and also suggestions for varying the ingredients according to what you can find readily in the supermarket or already in your cupboard. And, as always in the books of this series, you'll find a recommendation from Richard Marmet, president of Best Cellars, for an inexpensive everyday wine to complement each meal.

Judith Hill
Editor in Chief
FOOD & WINE Books

Before You Begin

You'll find test-kitchen tips and ideas for ingredient substitutions presented with the individual recipes throughout the book. In this opening section, we've gathered information and tips that apply to all, or at least a substantial number, of the recipes. These are the facts and opinions that we'd like you to know before you use, and to keep in mind while you use, the recipes. We hope you'll read these pages prior to cooking from the book for the first time—and have kept the section short so that you can do so with ease. The culinary information here will help make your cooking quicker, simpler, and even tastier.

RECIPES PICTURED OPPOSITE: (top) pages 35, 133, 25; (center) pages 153, 53, 143; (bottom) pages 167, 111, 169

Substituting Parts—or Birds

If you like white meat and the recipe calls for dark (or vice versa), or if you want to interchange Cornish hens and chicken, by all means do so. Simply increase or decrease cooking time according to the times given in our chart. These guidelines are based on chickens that weigh 3 to 3½ pounds and Cornish hens of about 1¼ pounds. The cooking times are necessarily approximate, but they'll get you close to the mark.

INSTEAD OF	USE	COOKING METHOD	COOKING TIME
Legs			
4 whole bone-in legs	4 bone-in individual breasts	Roast, sauté, grill Simmer	5 min. less 10 min. less
8 bone-in thighs or drumsticks	4 bone-in individual breasts	Roast, sauté, grill Simmer	4 min. less 8 min. less
4 boneless, skinless thighs	4 boneless, skinless breasts	Sauté, grill Simmer	4 min. less 5 min. less
Cut-up boneless, skinless thighs	Cut-up boneless, skinless breasts	All methods	1 to 2 min. less
Breasts			
4 bone-in individual breasts	4 whole bone-in legs	Roast, sauté, grill Simmer	5 min. more 10 min. more
4 bone-in individual breasts	8 bone-in thighs or drumsticks	Roast, sauté, grill Simmer	4 min. more 8 min. more
4 boneless, skinless breasts	4 boneless, skinless thighs	Sauté, grill Simmer	4 min. more 5 min. more
Cut-up boneless, skinless breasts	Cut-up boneless, skinless thighs	All methods	1 to 2 min. more

Wings	2 pounds wings	4 bone-in individual breasts	Roast, sauté, grill	2 to 5 min. more
	2 pounds wings	8 thighs or drumsticks	Roast, sauté, grill	5 to 10 min. more
Whole or Half Chicken	1 chicken	2 Cornish hens	Roast	15 min. less
	2 chicken halves	4 Cornish-hen halves	Grill	10 min. less
Cornish Hens	2 Cornish hens	1 chicken	Roast	15 min. more
	4 Cornish-hen halves	2 chicken halves	Grill	10 min. more
Turkey	Turkey cutlets	Chicken cutlets	Sauté, grill	Same
	Turkey sausage	Chicken sausage	Sauté, grill	Same
	Ground turkey	Ground chicken	Sauté, grill	Same

Essential Ingredient Information

Broth, Chicken
We tested all of the recipes in this book using canned low-sodium chicken broth. You can almost always substitute regular for low-sodium broth; just cut back on the salt in the recipe. And if you keep homemade stock in your freezer, by all means feel free to use it. We aren't suggesting that it won't work as well, only that we know the dishes taste delicious even when made with canned broth.

Butter
Our recipes don't specify whether to use salted or unsalted butter. We generally use unsalted, but in these savory dishes, it really won't make a big difference which type you use.

Coconut Milk
Coconut milk is the traditional liquid used in many Thai and Indian curries. Make sure you buy *unsweetened* canned coconut milk, not cream of coconut, which is used primarily for piña coladas. Heavy cream can be substituted in many recipes.

Garlic
The size of garlic cloves varies tremendously. When we call for one minced or chopped clove, we expect you to get about three-quarters of a teaspoon.

Mustard
When we call for mustard, we mean Dijon or grainy. We never, ever mean yellow ballpark mustard.

Nuts
Our quick pantry wouldn't be complete without several kinds of nuts. Keep in mind that nuts have a high percentage of oil and can turn rancid quickly. We store ours in the freezer to keep them fresh.

Oil
Cooking oil in these recipes refers to readily available, reasonably priced nut, seed, or vegetable oil with a high smoking point, such as peanut, sunflower, canola, safflower, or corn oil. These can be heated to about 400° before they begin to smoke, break down, and develop an unpleasant flavor.

Olives

If your store doesn't sell olives from big, open barrels, opt for the kind in jars. The canned version gives you only the slightest hint of what a real olive might taste like.

Parsley

Many of our recipes call for chopped fresh parsley. The flat-leaf variety has a stronger flavor than the curly, and we use it most of the time, but unless the type is specified, you can use either.

Pepper

■ There's nothing like fresh-ground pepper. If you've been using preground, buy a pepper mill, fill it, and give it a grind. You'll never look back.

■ To measure your just-ground pepper more easily, become familiar with your own mill; each produces a different amount per turn. You'll probably find that ten to fifteen grinds produces one-quarter teaspoon of pepper, and then you can count on that forever after.

Sausages, Chicken and Turkey

While testing recipes for this book, we found tremendous differences in the quality and flavor of chicken and turkey sausages. Try various kinds to find your favorite.

Tomatoes, Canned

In some recipes, we call for "crushed tomatoes in thick puree." Depending on the brand, this mix of crushed tomatoes and tomato puree may be labeled crushed tomatoes with puree, with added puree, in tomato puree, thick style, or in thick puree. You can use any of these.

Wine, Dry White

Leftover wine is ideal for cooking. It seems a shame to open a fresh bottle for just a few spoonfuls. Another solution is to keep dry vermouth on hand. You can use whatever quantity is needed; the rest will keep indefinitely.

Zest

Citrus zest—the colored part of the peel, without any of the white pith—adds tremendous flavor to many a dish. Remove the zest from the fruit using either a grater or a zester. A zester is a small, inexpensive, and extremely handy tool. It has little holes that remove just the zest in fine ribbons. A zester is quick, easy to clean, and never scrapes your knuckles.

Faster, Better, Easier
TEST-KITCHEN TIPS

Defrosting chicken

We prefer to use fresh chicken, which always has juicier meat than frozen, but everybody freezes chicken at some time or another. When you do, remember that the method of defrosting affects the texture. We tested common methods on frozen chicken quarters.

■**Micowave:** *Quickest. Good quality.* We microwaved quartered chickens on the defrost setting for twenty-two minutes. When roasted, the meat wasn't quite as juicy as fresh but was still moist. Just be sure to keep an eye on the chicken while it's defrosting; don't let it cook.

■**Refrigerator:** *Slowest. Best quality.* Defrosting chicken in the refrigerator results in juicy meat, most like that of fresh. The only problem is that you need to think ahead; quartered chickens take a good twenty-four hours to defrost.

■**Warm running water:** *Least successful.* We ran warm water over the frozen chicken quarters for forty-five minutes to defrost. When cooked, the chicken was dry and stringy. We don't recommend this method.

Measuring spoons

We've found that measuring spoons with well rounded bottoms are the most accurate. Avoid the ones that are extremely shallow; they can be off by almost 50 percent.

Don't crowd chicken when browning

To brown chicken, use a pan large enough to hold all the pieces with at least half an inch between them. We recommend a ten-inch frying pan or pot. When chicken is crowded, the heat drops, and the pieces stew rather than brown. If your pan isn't wide enough, brown the chicken in two batches.

Quick kitchen method for carving chicken

To cut up a roast chicken quickly, use primarily your hands and a pair of scissors. We like Joyce Chen scissors, which are ideally engineered with large, round handles enclosed in plastic and short, sharp blades.

■**Breasts:** Start with a knife. Cut along one side of the breast bone and then slide the knife blade along the bones, cutting the meat off the bone as you go. After that use scissors. Break the wing joint attached to the bird and cut through it so that the wing stays attached to the breast meat. Cut the breast in half crosswise. Do the same with the other breast.

■**Legs:** Bend each leg back exposing the joint. Break the joint and then cut through it and along the backbone to release the leg from the carcass. Cut it into drumstick and thigh.

Avoid cooking poultry too long

Perfectly cooked poultry is juicy, tender, and tempting. Unfortunately, once overcooked, it's tough and dry. The breast is particularly susceptible to overcooking, not to mention diced chicken or turkey.

■ **Chicken breasts:** Nothing beats boneless, skinless breasts for fast cooking. So we have loads of recipes for them in this book, most of which require only ten minutes cooking time. Don't allow the breasts to overcook. Without the protection of the bone, they quickly become dry and disappointing.

■ **Turkey cutlets:** Cut from the breast, these are usually about one-quarter inch thick. Cooking takes one to two minutes per side at the most (rarely longer than three minutes total). If you cook them longer, they will be dry. We know it's hard to make yourself take a cutlet out of the pan almost as soon as you put it in, but trust us, you'll be glad you did.

■ **Diced poultry:** Small pieces of chicken or turkey can turn into hard little balls in a flash. Simmer or poach diced poultry at a low temperature. Never allow the liquid to boil, which would make the meat fibrous and dry.

Oven accuracy

It's not unusual for the actual temperature in your oven to vary wildly from the setting. To save your roasted and baked chickens from disaster, invest in an oven thermometer, take your oven's temperature occasionally, and adjust the setting accordingly.

Yellow-skinned chicken

Some varieties of supermarket chicken have a yellow tint to their skin, a result of the birds' feed. We find the color doesn't affect flavor, but the golden-hued poultry does seem to brown better than its fair-skinned counterpart.

Test for doneness

We think the classic method is the best way to check for doneness: Stick a small, sharp knife into the inside of the thigh. If the juices run clear, the chicken is done. If the juices are pink, continue cooking. This test applies to whole chickens, halves, and parts.

Golden-brown skin

If you're nearing the end of the roasting time and your chicken isn't quite as brown as you'd like, slide it under the broiler for the last few minutes of cooking. The skin should crisp right up.

The fastest way to peel garlic

Use a large knife to peel a garlic clove. Put the flat of the blade over the garlic and smack the blade with your fist or the heel of your hand. The clove will crack, and the skin will loosen and come off easily.

CHAPTER ONE

Sautés
&
Stir-Fries

PECAN-CRUSTED CHICKEN WITH MUSTARD SAUCE

Nutty sautéed chicken dipped in a creamy mustard sauce delivers nicely varied textures and flavors. Using cornstarch rather than flour makes the crust especially crisp.

WINE RECOMMENDATION
The combination of the sweet pecans and the assertive mustard sauce lends itself to either a crisp sparkling wine or a stainless-steel-fermented sauvignon blanc from California.

SERVES 4

- 1   cup pecans
- 2   tablespoons cornstarch
- 1   teaspoon dried thyme
- 1   teaspoon paprika
- 1½ teaspoons salt
-     Cayenne
- 1   egg
- 2   tablespoons water
- 4   boneless, skinless chicken breasts (about 1⅓ pounds in all)
- 3   tablespoons cooking oil
- 1   cup mayonnaise
- 2   tablespoons grainy or Dijon mustard
- ½   teaspoon white-wine vinegar
- ½   teaspoon sugar
- 2   tablespoons chopped fresh parsley

1. In a food processor, pulse the pecans with the cornstarch, thyme, paprika, 1¼ teaspoons of the salt, and ⅛ teaspoon cayenne until the nuts are chopped fine. Transfer the mixture to a medium bowl.

2. Whisk together the egg and the water in a small bowl. Dip each chicken breast into the egg mixture and then into the nut mixture.

3. In a large nonstick frying pan, heat the oil over moderate heat. Add the chicken to the pan and cook for 5 minutes. Turn and continue cooking until the chicken is golden brown and cooked through, 5 to 6 minutes longer.

4. Meanwhile, in a small bowl, combine the mayonnaise, mustard, vinegar, sugar, parsley, a pinch of cayenne, and the remaining ¼ teaspoon salt. Serve the chicken with the mustard dipping sauce.

MENU SUGGESTIONS

The crisp coating on the chicken invites a creamy potato gratin alongside. Green beans, perhaps sautéed in bacon fat, would taste great, too.

SAUTÉED CHICKEN BREASTS WITH FENNEL AND ROSEMARY

The Mediterranean flavors of fennel, garlic, and rosemary are perfect with chicken. The fennel and chicken are sautéed and then briefly braised in chicken broth, which becomes a tasty light sauce.

WINE RECOMMENDATION
The fennel and the rosemary will pair especially nicely with a full-bodied red wine that has a hint of sweetness, such as a Rioja from Spain.

SERVES 4

2   tablespoons olive oil

1   large fennel bulb (about 1¼ pounds), cut into ½-inch slices

2   teaspoons dried rosemary, crumbled

½   teaspoon salt

½   cup canned low-sodium chicken broth or homemade stock

4   boneless, skinless chicken breasts (about 1⅓ pounds in all)

¼   teaspoon fresh-ground black pepper

2   cloves garlic, minced

2   tablespoons chopped flat-leaf parsley

1. In a large nonstick frying pan, heat 1 tablespoon of the oil over moderately high heat. Add the fennel, 1 teaspoon of the rosemary, and ¼ teaspoon of the salt. Cook, stirring frequently, until the fennel is golden brown and almost done, about 12 minutes. Add the broth and bring to a boil. Cover, reduce the heat and simmer until the fennel is tender, about 3 minutes. Remove the fennel and the cooking liquid from the pan.

2. Wipe out the pan and heat the remaining 1 tablespoon oil over moderate heat. Season the chicken with the remaining ¼ teaspoon salt and ⅛ teaspoon of the pepper. Add the chicken to the pan with the remaining 1 teaspoon of rosemary and cook until brown, about 5 minutes. Turn and cook until almost done, about 3 minutes longer. Add the garlic; cook, stirring, for 30 seconds. Add the fennel and its cooking liquid and the remaining ⅛ teaspoon pepper. Bring to a simmer. Cover the pan and remove from the heat. Let steam 5 minutes. Stir in the parsley.

MENU SUGGESTIONS

Soft polenta is an appropriate accompaniment to this Italian-style dish. Mashed potatoes are another good match.

CHICKEN CHASSEUR

A French classic that never seems to go out of style, this dish combines mushrooms and chicken in a tomato and white-wine sauce. The name, literally *hunter's chicken*, harks back to a time when game birds and mushrooms from the woods were a natural autumn combination.

WINE RECOMMENDATION
This earthy dish is perfectly suited to the rustic charms of a country red wine from south-western France. Look for a bottle from one of the various appellations in that region, such as Cahors, Madiran, or Bergerac.

SERVES 4

1 tablespoon cooking oil

4 bone-in chicken breasts (about 2¼ pounds in all)

1 teaspoon salt

½ teaspoon fresh-ground black pepper

1 tablespoon butter

1 onion, chopped

¾ pound mushrooms, sliced

2 cloves garlic, minced

1½ teaspoons flour

6 tablespoons dry vermouth or dry white wine

⅔ cup canned low-sodium chicken broth or homemade stock

1 cup canned crushed tomatoes, drained

¼ teaspoon dried thyme

2 tablespoons chopped fresh parsley

1. In a large, deep frying pan, heat the oil over moderately high heat. Season the chicken with ¼ teaspoon each of the salt and pepper and add to the pan. Cook until browned, turning, about 8 minutes in all. Remove. Pour off all but 1 tablespoon fat from the pan.

2. Add the butter to the pan and reduce the heat to moderately low. Add the onion and cook, stirring occasionally, until translucent, about 5 minutes. Raise the heat to moderately high. Add the mushrooms, garlic, and ¼ teaspoon of the salt. Cook, stirring frequently, until the vegetables are browned, about 5 minutes.

3. Add the flour and cook, stirring, for 30 seconds. Stir in the vermouth and bring back to a simmer. Stir in the broth, tomatoes, thyme, and the remaining ½ teaspoon salt. Add the chicken and any accumulated juices. Reduce the heat; simmer, covered, until the chicken is done, about 10 minutes. Stir in the parsley and the remaining ¼ teaspoon pepper.

SAUTÉED CHICKEN BREASTS WITH TARRAGON CREAM SAUCE

Simple sautés such as this are perfect for quick meals. The sauce has a delicate tarragon flavor; thyme would also be a good herb to try here.

WINE RECOMMENDATION
The richness of the cream sauce will contrast well with a fresh white wine from the north of Italy. Try a tocai friulano, pinot grigio, or pinot bianco from an area such as Collio or the Alto Adige.

SERVES 4

2   tablespoons butter

4   boneless, skinless chicken breasts (about 1⅓ pounds in all)

¾   teaspoon salt

¼   teaspoon fresh-ground black pepper

2   tablespoons chopped onion

1   tablespoon flour

1   cup dry white wine

½   teaspoon dried tarragon, or 1½ teaspoons chopped fresh tarragon

½   cup heavy cream

1. In a medium frying pan, heat the butter over moderate heat. Season the chicken with ¼ teaspoon of the salt and the pepper and add it to the pan. Cook the chicken until brown, about 5 minutes. Turn and cook until just done, 4 to 5 minutes longer. Remove the chicken from the pan and put it in a warm spot.

2. Reduce the heat to moderately low. Stir in the onion and cook until starting to soften, about 2 minutes. Sprinkle the flour over the onion and stir to combine. Increase the heat to moderate; whisk in the wine and the tarragon, and cook until the sauce starts to thicken, about 2 minutes. Stir in the cream, the remaining ½ teaspoon salt, and any accumulated chicken juices. Serve the sauce over the chicken.

MENU SUGGESTIONS

Rice along with a simple vegetable such as steamed asparagus or sautéed zucchini and carrots would round out the meal nicely.

CORNMEAL-CRUSTED CHICKEN WITH GOAT-CHEESE AND SAUSAGE STUFFING

Bite through the crunchy coating and juicy meat of these chicken breasts and you'll be surprised by a soft, creamy goat-cheese center with a hint of spicy cayenne.

WINE RECOMMENDATION
There's a lot going on in this dish, from the Italian sausage to the acidic goat cheese and the crunchy cornmeal. A light, slightly chilled pinot noir from Burgundy in France or from Oregon has the fruitiness and acidity to make a perfect partner.

SERVES 4

5½   ounces goat cheese, crumbled

½   pound mild Italian sausage, casings removed, meat crumbled and cooked

¼   teaspoon cayenne

½   teaspoon salt

2   tablespoons chopped fresh parsley

4   boneless, skinless chicken breasts (about 1⅓ pounds in all)

1   egg

1   tablespoon water

¾   cup cornmeal

¼   teaspoon fresh-ground black pepper

3   tablespoons cooking oil

1. In a small bowl, combine the goat cheese, sausage, cayenne, ¼ teaspoon of the salt, and the parsley.

2. With a sharp knife, make an incision along the side of each chicken breast and cut into the middle, making a pocket without cutting through the edges. Fill each breast with the goat-cheese mixture and pinch the cut side of the breast together to seal in the stuffing.

3. In a small bowl, whisk the egg with the water. Mix the cornmeal with the remaining ¼ teaspoon salt and the pepper. Dip each chicken breast in the cornmeal mixture to coat lightly, then into the egg mixture, and then back in the cornmeal.

4. In a large frying pan, heat the oil over moderately high heat. Add the chicken and cook for 5 minutes. Turn and continue cooking until golden brown and cooked through, about 5 minutes longer.

MENU SUGGESTIONS

Creamy mashed potatoes and a simple green vegetable are delicious with this crisp chicken.

POTATO, MUSHROOM, AND CHICKEN HASH

Always a brunch favorite, hash is a hearty dinner option as well. You might top each serving with a fried egg. The yolk makes a silky sauce for every bite it touches.

WINE RECOMMENDATION
This satisfying dish will go with different drinks depending on the time of day. For brunch, try a mimosa (orange juice and sparkling wine). For dinner, serve a light, young Bordeaux from the Médoc in France.

SERVES 4

2	pounds boiling potatoes, peeled and cut into ¾-inch pieces
4	tablespoons cooking oil
1	onion, chopped
2	cloves garlic, chopped
½	pound mushrooms, cut into ½-inch pieces
1⅓	pounds boneless, skinless chicken breasts (about 4), cut into ½-inch pieces
1	teaspoon salt
¼	teaspoon fresh-ground black pepper
½	teaspoon dried thyme
¼	cup heavy cream
2	tablespoons chopped fresh parsley

1. Put the potatoes in a medium saucepan of salted water. Bring to a boil and simmer until almost tender, about 5 minutes. Drain.

2. In a large nonstick frying pan, heat 1 tablespoon of the oil over moderate heat. Add the onion, garlic, and mushrooms and cook, stirring occasionally, until the mushrooms are browned, about 6 minutes. Add the chicken, ½ teaspoon of the salt, the pepper, and the thyme. Sauté until the chicken is almost cooked through, 3 to 4 minutes. Remove the mixture from the pan.

3. Wipe out the frying pan and then heat the remaining 3 tablespoons oil over moderately high heat. Add the drained potatoes and let cook, without stirring, for 6 minutes. Add the remaining ½ teaspoon salt, stir the potatoes, and cook until well browned, about 4 minutes longer. Stir in the chicken and mushrooms, the cream, and the parsley. Cook until just heated through, 1 to 2 minutes longer.

TEST-KITCHEN TIP

This is the perfect place to use leftover cooked turkey or chicken. Just toss it in at the end with the mushrooms.

KUNG PAO CHICKEN

Quick Asian stir-fries make especially satisfying weeknight dinners. *Kung pao* is traditionally a seriously spicy dish, but we've given ours a moderate level of heat; feel free to adjust the quantity of red-pepper flakes to suit your taste. Serve with steamed rice.

WINE RECOMMENDATION
Since the chicken is salty and spicy, the drink's first job is to refresh. An aromatic white wine such as a sauvignon blanc from California or South Africa will do nicely, as will your favorite cold beer.

SERVES 4

1⅓ pounds boneless, skinless chicken breasts (about 4), cut into ½-inch pieces

5 tablespoons soy sauce

2 tablespoons sherry

1 tablespoon plus 2 teaspoons cornstarch

2 teaspoons sugar

2 tablespoons white-wine vinegar or rice vinegar

2 teaspoons Asian sesame oil

⅓ cup water

2 tablespoons cooking oil

½ cup peanuts

4 scallions, white bulbs and green tops cut separately into ½-inch pieces

¼ teaspoon dried red-pepper flakes

1. In a medium bowl, toss the chicken with 1 tablespoon of the soy sauce, 1 tablespoon of the sherry, and the 1 tablespoon cornstarch.

2. In a small bowl, combine the sugar, vinegar, sesame oil, water, and the remaining 4 tablespoons of soy sauce, 1 tablespoon of sherry, and 2 teaspoons cornstarch.

3. In a wok or large frying pan, heat 1 tablespoon of the oil over moderately high heat. Add the peanuts and stir-fry until light brown, about 30 seconds. Remove from the pan. Heat the remaining 1 tablespoon oil. Add the white part of the scallions and the red-pepper flakes to the pan and cook, stirring, for 30 seconds. Add the chicken with its marinade and cook, stirring, until almost done, 1 to 2 minutes. Add the soy-sauce mixture and the scallion tops and simmer until the chicken is just done, about 1 minute longer. Stir in the peanuts.

VARIATION

CASHEW CHICKEN

Substitute the same amount of cashews for the peanuts.

STIR-FRIED CHICKEN WITH CHINESE CABBAGE

A simple sauce of garlic, hot pepper, sherry, wine vinegar, and tomato adds intense flavor to this quick stir-fry, and it practically makes itself while the chicken and cabbage cook. Steamed rice is an ideal accompaniment.

WINE RECOMMENDATION
You need a straightforward white wine with plenty of acidity to survive the garlic, soy sauce, and hot pepper in this dish. A chenin blanc from the Loire Valley in France, particularly from Vouvray, Saumur, or Anjou, will be able to hold its own.

SERVES 4

1⅓ pounds boneless, skinless chicken breasts (about 4), cut into 1-inch pieces

1 tablespoon plus 4 teaspoons soy sauce

3 tablespoons dry sherry

¼ teaspoon cayenne

2 tablespoons cooking oil

1 onion, chopped

2 cloves garlic, minced

1 teaspoon ground coriander

1 tablespoon wine vinegar

½ head Chinese cabbage (about 1 pound), sliced

¾ cup drained sliced water chestnuts (from one 8-ounce can)

2 teaspoons tomato paste

¼ teaspoon dried red-pepper flakes

3 tablespoons water

3 tablespoons chopped cilantro or scallion tops

⅛ teaspoon salt

1. In a medium bowl, combine the chicken with the 1 tablespoon soy sauce, 1 tablespoon of the sherry, and the cayenne. Let marinate for 10 minutes.

2. In a wok or large frying pan, heat 1 tablespoon of the oil over moderately high heat. Add the chicken and cook, stirring, until almost done, 1 to 2 minutes. Remove.

3. Add the remaining 1 tablespoon oil to the pan. Add the onion, garlic, and coriander. Cook, stirring, until the onions are golden, about 4 minutes. Add the remaining 2 tablespoons sherry and the vinegar. Cook, stirring, 1 minute longer.

4. Add the cabbage, water chestnuts, the remaining 4 teaspoons soy sauce, the tomato paste, red-pepper flakes, and water and cook, stirring, for 3 minutes longer. Add the chicken and any accumulated juices, the cilantro, and the salt and cook, stirring, until the chicken is just done, 1 to 2 minutes longer.

CHICKEN PROVENÇAL

The flavors are bold in this French sauté with a sauce of tomatoes, garlic, rosemary, olives, and just enough anchovy paste to give the sauce depth.

WINE RECOMMENDATION

There are lots of interesting wines from the region of Provence that will be ideal with this dish. For a lighter, summer wine, look for a rosé from that region. If you prefer a red, try a Côtes de Provence.

SERVES 4

- 1 tablespoon cooking oil
- 1 chicken (about 3 to 3½ pounds), cut into eight pieces
- ¾ teaspoon salt
- ½ teaspoon fresh-ground black pepper
- 1 small onion, chopped
- 4 cloves garlic, minced
- ½ cup red wine
- 1½ cups canned crushed tomatoes with their juice
- ½ teaspoon dried rosemary
- ½ teaspoon dried thyme
- ⅓ cup black olives, such as Niçoise or Kalamata, halved and pitted
- 1 teaspoon anchovy paste

1. In a large, deep frying pan, heat the oil over moderately high heat. Season the chicken with ¼ teaspoon each of the salt and pepper and put it in the pan. Cook the chicken until browned, turning, about 8 minutes in all. Remove the chicken from the pan. Pour off all but 1 tablespoon fat from the pan.

2. Reduce the heat to moderately low. Add the onion and the garlic and cook, stirring occasionally, until the onion starts to soften, about 3 minutes. Add the wine to the pan and simmer until reduced to about ¼ cup, 1 to 2 minutes. Add the tomatoes, rosemary, thyme, olives, anchovy paste, and the remaining ½ teaspoon salt and simmer for 5 minutes.

3. Add the chicken thighs and drumsticks and any accumulated juices. Reduce the heat to low and simmer, covered, for 10 minutes. Add the breasts and cook until the chicken is just done, about 10 minutes more. Add the remaining ¼ teaspoon pepper.

MENU SUGGESTIONS

Simple roasted new potatoes or boiled green beans would be excellent with the gutsy flavors here.

RUSSIAN-STYLE CHICKEN CUTLETS

So simple and so good—these cutlets are a case where the whole is greater than the sum of the parts. Ground chicken is often disappointingly dry, but here a bit of butter and cream keep the meat moist.

WINE RECOMMENDATION
The butteriness of the juicy cutlets contrasts beautifully with the racy freshness of an uncomplicated red wine. A Beaujolais from France or a merlot from Trentino in Northern Italy will be perfect.

SERVES 4

2 slices good-quality white bread, crusts removed

¼ cup half-and-half

1 pound ground chicken

1 egg

½ teaspoon salt

¼ teaspoon fresh-ground black pepper

½ teaspoon dried dill

5 tablespoons butter, 3 of them at room temperature

1 cup dry bread crumbs

2 tablespoons cooking oil

1. Break the bread into pieces. In a large bowl, soak the bread in the half-and-half until the liquid is absorbed, about 2 minutes. Mix in the chicken, egg, salt, pepper, dill, and the 3 tablespoons room-temperature butter. Put in the freezer for about 10 minutes to firm up.

2. Remove the chicken mixture from the freezer; it will still be very soft. Form the mixture into four oval cutlets and coat them with the bread crumbs.

3. In a large, nonstick frying pan, heat the remaining 2 tablespoons butter and the oil over moderate heat. Cook the cutlets until golden brown and just done, 4 to 5 minutes per side.

VARIATION

ITALIAN-STYLE CHICKEN CUTLETS

Omit the dill. Use half bread crumbs, half grated Parmesan cheese to coat the cutlets.

MENU SUGGESTIONS

Sautéed mushrooms are the traditional Russian accompaniment to chicken cutlets. Beets, glazed carrots, and mashed potatoes are other excellent possibilities.

CHICKEN LIVERS WITH CARAMELIZED ONIONS AND MADEIRA

Rich-tasting caramelized onions combined with Madeira make a spectacular sauce for chicken livers. Serve with rice or over toast so you won't miss a single drop.

WINE RECOMMENDATION
The rich and luscious Madeira sauce is ideal with fruity, spicy grenache-based wines. A Gigondas or a Côtes-du-Rhône from the Rhône Valley in France or a bottle of grenache from California would be appropriate.

SERVES 4

3 tablespoons cooking oil

3 onions, sliced thin (about 4 cups)

¾ teaspoon salt

¼ teaspoon fresh-ground black pepper

1¼ pounds chicken livers, each cut in half

½ cup Madeira

1 hard-cooked egg, chopped

2 tablespoons chopped fresh parsley

1. In a large frying pan, heat 2 tablespoons of the oil over moderate heat. Add the onions, ½ teaspoon of the salt, and ⅛ teaspoon of the pepper. Cook, stirring frequently, until the onions are well browned, about 15 minutes. Remove the onions from the pan and put on a serving platter or individual plates.

2. In the same frying pan, heat the remaining 1 tablespoon oil over moderately high heat.

Season the chicken livers with the remaining ¼ teaspoon salt and ⅛ teaspoon pepper. Put the livers in the pan, in two batches if necessary, and cook for 2 minutes. Turn and cook until browned, about 2 minutes longer. The livers should still be pink inside. Remove the chicken livers from the pan and put them on top of the onions.

3. Return the pan to the heat and add the Madeira. Boil rapidly, scraping the bottom of the pan to dislodge any brown bits, for 1 minute. Pour the sauce over the livers and the onions. Top with the egg and parsley.

VARIATIONS

CHICKEN LIVERS WITH CARAMELIZED ONIONS AND SHERRY

Use ½ cup of dry sherry instead of the Madeira.

CHICKEN LIVERS WITH CARAMELIZED ONIONS AND PORT

Use ½ cup of port instead of the Madeira.

SAUTÉED CHICKEN LIVERS WITH RAISINS AND PINE NUTS

Sicily is the inspiration for chicken livers in a wine sauce redolent of garlic and studded with raisins and pine nuts. The livers are delicious over polenta—better yet, crisp fried polenta. Or serve them on a bed of buttered noodles or on toast.

WINE RECOMMENDATION
Try matching the savory tastes of this Sicilian-flavored dish with a rustic red wine that hails from the same region. Or serve the easy-to-find Salice Salentino from Apulia, also in Southern Italy.

SERVES 4

⅓ cup pine nuts

⅓ cup raisins

¾ cup canned low-sodium chicken broth
    or homemade stock

¾ cup dry vermouth or dry white wine

2 tablespoons butter

2 tablespoons olive oil

1¼ pounds chicken livers, each cut in half

½ teaspoon salt

¼ teaspoon fresh-ground black pepper

4 cloves garlic, minced

1½ teaspoons flour

3 tablespoons chopped flat-leaf parsley

1. Heat the oven to 350°. Toast the pine nuts in the oven until they are golden brown, about 8 minutes.

2. In a small stainless-steel saucepan, combine the raisins, broth, and vermouth. Bring to a boil and simmer until reduced to about ¾ cup, about 8 minutes. Set aside.

3. In a large frying pan, melt 1 tablespoon of the butter with 1 tablespoon of the oil over moderately high heat. Season the livers with ¼ teaspoon of the salt and ⅛ teaspoon of the pepper and cook, in two batches if necessary, until almost done, about 3 minutes. The livers should still be quite pink inside. Remove them from the pan.

4. Add the remaining 1 tablespoon oil and 1 tablespoon butter to the pan and reduce the heat to moderately low. Add the garlic and cook, stirring, for 30 seconds. Add the flour and cook, stirring, for 15 seconds longer. Stir in the raisin-and-vermouth mixture and the remaining ¼ teaspoon salt and ⅛ teaspoon pepper. Bring to a simmer, scraping the bottom of the pan to dislodge any brown bits. Add the livers and any accumulated juices, the pine nuts, and the parsley and simmer until the livers are just done, about 1 minute longer.

TURKEY SCALOPPINE WITH TOMATOES AND CAPERS

Searing the turkey for two minutes and then stirring together a simple pan sauce—that's all it takes to make this Italian-inspired dish.

WINE RECOMMENDATION

An Italian wine is a natural here; a bottle of sangiovese-based Chianti from Tuscany in Italy would be perfect. Another alternative, also made from sangiovese grapes, is a Rosso di Montalcino.

SERVES 4

2 tablespoons cooking oil

4 turkey cutlets (about 1¼ pounds in all)

½ teaspoon salt

¼ teaspoon fresh-ground black pepper

⅓ cup flour

⅓ cup dry white wine

½ cup canned low-sodium chicken broth or homemade stock

½ teaspoon dried marjoram

½ cup canned crushed tomatoes in thick puree

1 tablespoon butter

2 tablespoons capers

1. In a large nonstick frying pan, heat the oil over moderately high heat. Season the turkey with ¼ teaspoon of the salt and the pepper. Dredge the turkey in the flour and then shake off any excess. Cook the cutlets until just done, 1 to 2 minutes per side. Remove from the pan and cover loosely with foil to keep warm.

2. Decrease the heat to moderate. Add the wine to the pan and cook, stirring to dislodge any brown bits that cling to the bottom of the pan, for 1 minute. Add the broth and marjoram and simmer for 2 minutes longer. Stir in the tomatoes, butter, and the remaining ¼ teaspoon salt. Simmer until starting to thicken, about 4 minutes. Stir in the capers. Spoon the sauce over the scaloppine.

MENU SUGGESTIONS

Keep it simple and Italian; either sautéed spinach or spaghetti with garlic and oil would fill the bill.

TURKEY WITH BACON AND GREENS

Thin turkey cutlets are sautéed quickly and served with tender Swiss chard and a sour-cream-based sauce. Feel free to use chicken breasts instead of turkey, or spinach in place of the Swiss chard.

WINE RECOMMENDATION
This quick sauté will be great with a fairly acidic red wine, which will cut through the richness of the bacon and match the acidity of the sour cream. Look for a Beaujolais or try a grenache-based wine from California. Serve it slightly chilled.

SERVES 4

1½ pounds Swiss chard, long stems removed, leaves chopped and washed well

1 tablespoon water

¼ pound sliced bacon, cut into ¼-inch strips

1 onion, chopped

2 cloves garlic, chopped

4 turkey cutlets (about 1¼ pounds in all)

¾ teaspoon salt

¼ teaspoon fresh-ground black pepper

½ cup sour cream

1. Put the Swiss chard and the water in a medium pot. In a large nonstick frying pan, cook the bacon until crisp. Drain on paper towels. Pour off and reserve all but 1 tablespoon of the bacon fat, which you should leave in the pan.

2. Put the pan with the one tablespoon of fat over moderately low heat. Add the onion and cook, stirring occasionally, until translucent, about 5 minutes. Add the garlic and cook, stirring 30 seconds longer. Add the mixture to the Swiss chard. Bring the water to a simmer, cover, and cook over low heat until the greens are wilted and tender, about 5 minutes.

3. Meanwhile, heat 2 tablespoons of the reserved bacon fat in the frying pan over moderately high heat. Season the turkey cutlets with ¼ teaspoon of the salt and the pepper. Cook until just done, 1 to 2 minutes per side. Remove the cutlets from the pan so that they don't overcook.

4. Remove the Swiss chard from the heat. Stir in the sour cream and the remaining ½ teaspoon salt. Remove the greens from the pot with a slotted spoon, leaving the sauce. Divide the greens among four plates. Top each pile of chard with a turkey cutlet. Spoon some of the sauce over the top and sprinkle with the bacon.

MENU SUGGESTIONS

Since the recipe includes a vegetable, you can finish off the meal simply with steak fries or buttered orzo.

TURKEY WITH WALNUT PARMESAN SAUCE

Ground walnuts thicken this unique sauce and give it both a subtle nuttiness and an appealing creamy texture, both of which are perfect with turkey.

WINE RECOMMENDATION
The walnuts will stand up to a bold red wine. Try one from the Northern Rhône in France or a California cabernet sauvignon.

SERVES 4

- ⅓ cup walnuts
- 2 tablespoons butter
- ½ cup chopped onion
- 2 cloves garlic, chopped
- Pinch ground cloves
- Pinch ground cinnamon
- Pinch cayenne
- ½ teaspoon salt
- 1½ teaspoons flour
- ¾ cup canned low-sodium chicken broth or homemade stock
- ½ teaspoon lemon juice
- 1½ tablespoons grated Parmesan cheese
- 2 tablespoons chopped fresh parsley
- 1 tablespoon cooking oil
- 4 turkey cutlets (about 1¼ pounds in all)
- ¼ teaspoon fresh-ground black pepper

1. Grind ¼ cup of the walnuts to a powder in a food processor. In a small saucepan, melt the butter over moderately low heat. Add the onion; cook until translucent, about 5 minutes. Add the garlic and cook, stirring, 30 seconds longer. Stir in the cloves, cinnamon, cayenne, and ¼ teaspoon of the salt. Add the flour and stir to combine. Whisk in the broth and simmer until starting to thicken, about 3 minutes. Add the ground walnuts and simmer 1 minute longer. Remove from the heat and stir in the lemon juice, Parmesan, and parsley.

2. In a large nonstick frying pan, heat the oil over moderately high heat. Season the turkey with the remaining ¼ teaspoon salt and the pepper. Cook the turkey cutlets until just done, 1 to 2 minutes per side. Serve with the walnut sauce, sprinkling the additional nuts over the top.

MENU SUGGESTIONS

Roasted asparagus and sautéed peppers are vegetables that taste particularly good with both walnuts and Parmesan cheese.

CHAPTER TWO

Roasted, Baked & Grilled

ROAST CHICKEN WITH ROSEMARY AND LEMON

Lemon zest and rosemary placed in the cavity of the bird permeate the meat as it cooks and give a subtle Mediterranean accent to the pan juices. We call for dried rosemary, but if you have fresh, use several sprigs in place of the one tablespoon.

WINE RECOMMENDATION
A straightforward gulpable red wine will pair best with this aromatic dish. Try a Chianti from the Italian region of Tuscany.

SERVES 4

1   chicken (3 to 3½ pounds)
1   tablespoon dried rosemary
    Salt
    Fresh-ground black pepper
4   3-inch-long strips lemon zest
1   small onion, quartered
1   tablespoon olive oil
1   tablespoon plus ¼ teaspoon lemon juice
½   cup water

1. Heat the oven to 425°. Rub the cavity of the chicken with the dried rosemary, ¼ teaspoon salt, and ⅛ teaspoon pepper and then stuff with the strips of lemon zest and the quartered onion. Twist the wings behind the back of the chicken and tie the legs together. Put the chicken, breast-side up, in a roasting pan. Coat the chicken with the oil and sprinkle it with ¼ teaspoon of salt, ⅛ teaspoon of pepper, and the 1 tablespoon lemon juice.

2. Roast the chicken until it is just done, 50 to 60 minutes. Transfer the bird to a plate and leave to rest in a warm spot for about 10 minutes.

3. Meanwhile, pour off the fat from the roasting pan. Set the pan over moderate heat and add the water. Bring to a boil, scraping the bottom of the pan to dislodge any brown bits. Boil until reduced to approximately ¼ cup, about 4 minutes. Add any accumulated juices from the chicken along with the remaining ¼ teaspoon lemon juice and a pinch each of salt and pepper. Serve the bird with the pan juices.

MENU SUGGESTIONS

The simplicity of this chicken means that an almost endless list of accompaniments will work well with it. Among the easiest are vegetables that you can roast in a separate pan alongside the chicken, such as potatoes, squash, asparagus, or fennel. Other good choices include rice, polenta, or mashed potatoes.

ROAST CHICKEN WITH CRANBERRY APPLE RAISIN CHUTNEY

Cranberries may call the holidays to mind, but this combination tastes great any time of year. You can serve the chutney warm or at room temperature; if there's any left over, use it to light up a chicken, turkey, or ham sandwich.

WINE RECOMMENDATION
This sweet, fruit-laden dish is best with a wine that shares these characteristics, such as a slightly chilled bottle of Chinon from the Loire Valley in France or a dolcetto from Italy.

SERVES 4

1   chicken (3 to 3½ pounds)

   Salt

   Fresh-ground black pepper

4   3-inch-long strips orange zest

1   tablespoon olive oil

1   12-ounce package fresh or frozen cranberries (about 3 cups)

1   tart apple, such as Granny Smith, peeled, cored, and cut into ½-inch chunks

1   cup raisins

⅔   cup brown sugar

½   cup apple juice

4   teaspoons cider vinegar

¼   teaspoon ground ginger

½   cup orange juice (from about 1 orange)

1. Heat the oven to 425°. Rub the chicken cavity with ¼ teaspoon salt and ⅛ teaspoon pepper and put the orange zest inside. Twist the wings of the chicken behind the back and tie the legs together. Put the chicken, breast-side up, in a roasting pan. Coat the chicken with the oil and sprinkle with ¼ teaspoon salt and ⅛ teaspoon pepper. Roast the chicken until just done, 50 to 60 minutes.

2. Meanwhile, in a medium stainless-steel saucepan, bring the cranberries to a boil with the apple, raisins, brown sugar, apple juice, vinegar, ginger, ⅛ teaspoon salt, and ⅛ teaspoon pepper. Cover and simmer over moderate heat, stirring occasionally, until the liquid has thickened and the fruit is tender, about 15 minutes.

3. When the chicken is done, transfer the bird to a plate and leave to rest in a warm spot for about 10 minutes. Pour off the fat from the roasting pan. Set the pan over moderate heat and add the orange juice. Bring to a boil, scraping the bottom of the pan to dislodge any brown bits. Boil until reduced to approximately ¼ cup, about 4 minutes. Add any accumulated juices from the chicken and a pinch each of salt and pepper. Serve the chicken with the orange sauce and the chutney.

ROAST CHICKEN WITH
MAPLE PEPPER GLAZE AND SWEET POTATOES

You'll look forward to cool weather just so you can make this irresistible dish. The maple pepper glaze laced with bourbon gives the chicken an extra-crisp skin and drips down to flavor the sweet potatoes as they roast alongside. To gild the lily, add one cup of pecan halves to the potatoes about ten minutes before they're done.

WINE RECOMMENDATION
With ingredients like maple syrup, bourbon, and sweet potatoes, this dish should be matched with an all-American wine. The best choice is a fruity zinfandel from California.

SERVES 4

2   pounds sweet potatoes (about 3), peeled and cut into 1½-inch pieces

2   tablespoons cooking oil

1   teaspoon salt

1¼ teaspoons fresh-ground black pepper

1   chicken (3 to 3½ pounds)

1   tablespoon butter, cut into small pieces

6   tablespoons pure maple syrup

1½ tablespoons bourbon

1. Heat the oven to 425°. In a large roasting pan, toss the sweet potatoes with 1 tablespoon of the oil, ½ teaspoon of the salt, and ¼ teaspoon of the pepper. Push them to the edges of the pan, leaving a space in the center for the chicken.

2. Rub the cavity of the chicken with ¼ teaspoon of the salt and ⅛ teaspoon of the pepper.

Twist the wings behind the back and tie the legs together. Put the chicken, breast-side up, in the center of the roasting pan. Coat the chicken with the remaining tablespoon oil, sprinkle with the remaining ¼ teaspoon salt and ⅛ teaspoon of the pepper, and dot with the butter. Roast the chicken for 30 minutes.

3. Meanwhile, in a small bowl, combine the maple syrup, bourbon, and the remaining ¾ teaspoon pepper. Remove the roasting pan from the oven and stir the potatoes. Brush the chicken with about 2 tablespoons of the glaze and drizzle the potatoes with about ½ tablespoon of the glaze. Return the pan to the oven and cook, stirring the potatoes and brushing the chicken with the remaining glaze 2 more times, until the chicken and potatoes are just done, about 30 minutes longer. Transfer the bird and potatoes to a plate and leave to rest in a warm spot for about 10 minutes.

4. Meanwhile, pour off the fat from the roasting pan. Add any accumulated juices from the chicken to the liquid in the pan. Serve the chicken with the pan juices and sweet potatoes.

ROAST CORNISH HENS
WITH PANZANELLA STUFFING

Italian bread salad is the inspiration for this simple stuffing that bakes in a dish along-side the hens until crisp and golden brown.

WINE RECOMMENDATION
This rustic, Italian-influenced recipe will go nicely with an Italian red such as a Chianti Classico. It combines fruit flavors with the acidity to stand up to the strong ingredients here.

SERVES 4

1 1/2-pound loaf sourdough or firm country bread, cut into 1-inch cubes (about 8 cups)

2 Cornish hens

3 tablespoons olive oil

1 teaspoon salt
   Fresh-ground black pepper

1 tablespoon butter, cut into small pieces

2 cups drained diced canned tomatoes

3 cloves garlic, minced

6 tablespoons chopped flat-leaf parsley

2 teaspoons dried rosemary, crumbled, or
   2 tablespoons chopped fresh rosemary

1. Set the oven at 425°. Put the bread cubes in the oven while it heats and toast them until golden brown, about 6 minutes.

2. Twist the wings of the Cornish hens behind their backs and tie the legs together. Put the hens, breast-side up, in a roasting pan. Coat the hens with 1 tablespoon of the oil; sprinkle with 1/4 teaspoon of the salt and 1/8 teaspoon pepper. Dot with the butter. Roast the hens until just done, about 40 minutes.

3. Meanwhile, oil a deep 1-quart baking dish. In a large bowl, toss the tomatoes with the garlic, parsley, rosemary, the remaining 3/4 teaspoon salt, and 1/4 teaspoon pepper. Add the toasted bread cubes and the remaining 2 tablespoons oil and stir well to combine. Put the stuffing in the prepared baking dish and cover with a lid or with aluminum foil. Bake for 20 minutes. Remove the cover; bake until the stuffing is crisp and golden brown, about 12 minutes longer.

4. When the hens are done, transfer them to a plate and leave to rest in a warm spot for about 10 minutes. Pour off the fat from the roasting pan and add any accumulated juices from the hens. Cut the hens in half and serve with the stuffing and the pan juices.

MENU SUGGESTION

Only a green vegetable, perhaps broccoli rabe, is needed to complete the meal.

TURKEY BREAST
WITH MUSTARD SAGE CRUMBS

Seasoned bread crumbs form an appealing brown crust on this turkey breast that tastes as good as it looks. We developed it for quick weeknight cooking, but it would make a fine holiday feast for a small group.

WINE RECOMMENDATION
The mild flavors of this dish provide an opportunity to explore a full-flavored red wine. Try a bottle of easy-to-like, easy-to-drink zinfandel from California or a shiraz from Australia.

SERVES 4

½ cup dry bread crumbs
1½ teaspoons dried sage
¼ cup chopped fresh parsley
3 tablespoons melted butter
¾ teaspoon salt
1 2-pound boneless, skinless turkey breast
¼ teaspoon fresh-ground black pepper
1 tablespoon Dijon mustard

1. Heat the oven to 450°. In a small bowl, combine the bread crumbs, sage, parsley, butter, and ¼ teaspoon of the salt.

2. Season the turkey breast with the remaining ½ teaspoon salt and the pepper. Set the turkey breast in a roasting pan and then brush the top and the sides of the breast with the mustard. Pat the seasoned bread crumbs onto the mustard.

3. Roast the turkey for 20 minutes. Reduce the oven temperature to 375° and continue to roast the turkey breast until just done, 15 to 20 minutes longer. Transfer the turkey to a carving board and leave to rest in a warm spot for about 10 minutes. Cut the turkey into slices.

MENU SUGGESTIONS

A moist and creamy side dish—mashed potatoes or sweet potatoes, baked squash, or creamed corn or spinach—is the perfect foil for the turkey.

TEST-KITCHEN TIP

Sometimes boneless turkey breasts come rolled and tied like a roast. For this preparation, you'll want to unroll the breast and put it flat in the roasting pan, thereby cutting the cooking time significantly.

CHICKEN WITH WINE AND TARRAGON

Here's a delectable French classic that never seems to go out of style. The sauce takes only a few minutes to make, but if you prefer you can serve the chicken without it. Green beans are a good accompaniment.

WINE RECOMMENDATION
A full-bodied, rustic red wine from the south of France is a perfect choice for this traditional French dish. A Gigondas, Côtes-du-Rhône, or Crozes-Hermitage, each from the Rhône Valley, would be a good choice.

SERVES 4

3 tablespoons dry white wine or dry vermouth

2 teaspoons dried tarragon

1 chicken (3 to 3½ pounds), quartered

1 tablespoon olive oil

Salt

Fresh-ground black pepper

1 tablespoon butter, cut into 4 pieces

¼ cup water

1. Heat the oven to 375°. In a small glass or stainless-steel bowl, combine 2 tablespoons of the wine and ½ teaspoon of the dried tarragon. Set aside.

2. Coat the chicken with the olive oil and arrange the pieces, skin-side up, in a large roasting pan. Sprinkle the chicken pieces with the remaining 1 tablespoon wine and season with ¼ teaspoon salt and ⅛ teaspoon pepper. Top each piece of chicken with a piece of the butter.

3. Cook the chicken for 15 minutes and then sprinkle with the remaining 1½ teaspoons tarragon. Baste the chicken and cook until the breasts are just done, about 20 minutes longer. Remove the breasts and cook the legs until done, about 5 minutes longer. Remove the roasting pan from the oven; return the breasts to the pan.

4. Heat the broiler. Baste the chicken and then broil until the skin is golden brown, about 2 minutes. Transfer the chicken to a plate.

5. Pour off the fat from the roasting pan. Set the pan over moderate heat and add the reserved wine-and-tarragon mixture and the water. Bring to a boil, scraping the bottom of the pan to dislodge any brown bits. Boil until reduced to approximately 3 tablespoons, about 3 minutes. Add any accumulated juices from the chicken and a pinch each of salt and pepper. Spoon the sauce over the chicken.

CHICKEN WITH PORT AND FIGS

Dried figs are poached in port to make a luscious Portuguese-inspired sauce. Ruby port provides the best color, but tawny will also taste good.

WINE RECOMMENDATION
A Portuguese red wine such as a Dão, combining soft texture with full flavor, is a geographical match. The savory sauce would also go nicely with a fruity cabernet sauvignon or merlot from either California or Australia.

SERVES 4

8 dried figs, tough stems removed

1 cup water

²/₃ cup plus 1 tablespoon port

2 3-inch-long strips lemon zest

1 chicken (3 to 3½ pounds), quartered

1 tablespoon olive oil

  Salt

  Fresh-ground black pepper

1 tablespoon butter, cut into four pieces

1. Heat the oven to 375°. Pierce each fig three or four times with a paring knife. In a small stainless-steel saucepan, combine the figs, water, the ²/₃ cup port, and the lemon zest. Bring to a boil and simmer, covered, until tender, about 30 minutes. Discard the zest and reserve the poaching liquid. Cut the figs in half.

2. Meanwhile, coat the chicken with the oil and arrange the pieces, skin-side up, in a large roasting pan. Sprinkle the chicken with the remaining 1 tablespoon port and season with ¼ teaspoon salt and ⅛ teaspoon pepper. Top each piece of chicken with a piece of the butter. Cook until the breasts are just done, about 30 minutes. Remove the breasts and continue to cook the legs until done, about 5 minutes longer. Remove the roasting pan from the oven; return the breasts to the pan.

3. Heat the broiler. Broil the chicken until the skin is golden brown, about 2 minutes. Transfer the chicken to a plate.

4. Pour off the fat from the roasting pan. Set the pan over moderate heat and add the fig-poaching liquid. Bring to a boil, scraping the bottom of the pan to dislodge any brown bits. Boil until reduced to approximately ¼ cup, about 4 minutes. Add the figs, any accumulated juices from the chicken, and a pinch each of salt and pepper. Spoon the sauce over the chicken.

MENU SUGGESTION

A green vegetable, such as steamed broccoli, makes a quick and easy side dish.

Spiced Chicken Breasts with Dried Apricots

A paste made of ground sesame seeds, almonds, cumin, coriander, and oregano gives both the chicken and the apricots delicious flavor.

WINE RECOMMENDATION
A red or white wine with low tannin and plenty of fruit flavor will match the sweet, tangy apricots. For a red, a pinot noir from Oregon would be a good choice; for a white, a pinot blanc from Alsace in France.

SERVES 4

¾ cup dried apricots

1½ cups water

½ cup sliced almonds

⅓ cup sesame seeds

2 tablespoons ground cumin

2 tablespoons ground coriander

2 tablespoons paprika

2 tablespoons dried oregano
    Salt

¼ cup olive oil

2 tablespoons lemon juice

4 bone-in chicken breasts (about 2¼ pounds in all)

1. Heat the oven to 425°. In a small saucepan, combine the apricots and water. Bring to a boil, lower the heat, and then simmer, partially covered, for 10 minutes. Set aside.

2. Toast the almonds and sesame seeds in the oven until just beginning to brown, about 2 minutes. Transfer ⅓ cup of the almonds and ¼ cup of the sesame seeds to a blender; pulverize with the cumin, coriander, paprika, oregano, and ½ teaspoon salt. Put the mixture in a small bowl; stir in the oil and lemon juice to make a paste. Stir half of the paste into the apricots and water.

3. Put the chicken breasts in a small roasting pan, skin-side up, and coat with the remaining paste. Pour the apricot mixture around the chicken. Cook in the lower third of the oven until done, 20 to 25 minutes. If the chicken seems to be browning too quickly, cover the pan with aluminum foil the last 10 minutes of cooking.

4. Transfer the chicken to a plate. Spoon the fat from the pan. Serve the chicken topped with the apricots and any pan juices. Sprinkle the remaining almonds and sesame seeds over all.

Menu Suggestions

Steamed rice is an ideal accompaniment. So are roasted potatoes cooked alongside the chicken in a separate pan.

CHICKEN WITH BANANA CURRY SAUCE

Caribbean curries often have a mild sweetness, usually from fruit. The banana flavor here is very subtle; you needn't worry about your dinner tasting like dessert.

WINE RECOMMENDATION
A completely dry wine will taste coarse and acidic with the fruity and slightly sweet flavor here. Instead, choose a white with a touch of sweetness. An off-dry California chenin blanc, gewürztraminer, or riesling will hold its own nicely.

SERVES 4

2 large bananas, cut into pieces

2 tablespoons curry powder

2 teaspoons ground coriander

1 teaspoon dry mustard

3 tablespoons butter

   Grated zest of 1 lime

4 teaspoons lime juice

1¼ teaspoons salt

½ teaspoon fresh-ground black pepper

¾ cup water, more if needed

4 bone-in chicken breasts (about 2¼ pounds in all), skin removed

1 tablespoon fresh chopped parsley (optional)

1. Heat the oven to 450°. In a food processor or blender, puree the bananas, curry powder, coriander, dry mustard, butter, lime zest, lime juice, salt, pepper, and ¼ cup of the water.

2. Make a few deep cuts in each chicken breast and put the breasts in a roasting pan. Pour the curry sauce over the chicken, making sure the sauce gets into the cuts. Roast in the bottom third of the oven until the chicken is just done, about 20 minutes.

3. Remove the roasting pan from the oven and remove the chicken breasts from the pan. There should be plenty of thick sauce in the bottom of the pan. Set the pan over moderate heat and whisk in the remaining ½ cup water. Continue to whisk until the sauce is heated through, adding more water if you want a thinner sauce. Serve the chicken breasts with the sauce over them. Sprinkle with parsley if you like.

MENU SUGGESTION

Be sure to have plenty of rice ready to catch the generous quantity of sauce.

ORANGE-GLAZED CHICKEN WINGS

Roll up your sleeves and dig into dinner! Orange juice and zest, soy sauce, and plenty of garlic coat these wings with fabulous flavor.

WINE RECOMMENDATION
Sweet, salty, and hot, this dish really needs a wine with good acidity, moderate alcohol, and just a touch of sweetness. Look for a low-alcohol German kabinett riesling or a semi-dry riesling from the Finger Lakes region of New York.

SERVES 4

1 cup fresh orange juice (from about 2 oranges)

2 tablespoons grated orange zest (from about 3 oranges)

6 cloves garlic, minced

¼ cup soy sauce

1 tablespoon brown sugar

1½ teaspoons salt

½ teaspoon fresh-ground black pepper

4 pounds chicken wings

1. Heat the oven to 400°. In a large bowl, combine the orange juice with the orange zest, garlic, soy sauce, brown sugar, salt, and pepper. Add the chicken wings and toss to coat.

2. On two large baking sheets, arrange the wings in a single layer. Reserve ¼ cup of the orange mixture and spoon the rest of the mixture over the wings. Bake for 20 minutes. Turn the wings over and baste them with the reserved orange mixture. Cook until just done, about 10 minutes longer.

MENU SUGGESTIONS

Serve this finger food with a vegetable that you can also eat with your hands, such as strips of raw fennel or jicama.

TEST-KITCHEN TIP

When you grate the orange zest, remove only the orange layer of the skin, leaving the bitter white pith behind.

JERK CHICKEN

Jamaicans love this sweet-and-spicy rub on both chicken and meat. Our rub is a little less fiery than the traditional version, but if you'd like to kick the heat up a notch, just add more cayenne pepper.

WINE RECOMMENDATION
The strong flavors in this recipe will be best with a refreshing wine that combines low alcohol and good acidity. Try a slightly chilled Beaujolais from France. Or open a cold bottle of a light-bodied beer.

SERVES 4

- 3 scallions including green tops, chopped
- 2 cloves garlic, chopped
- 1 tablespoon ground allspice
- 1 tablespoon dried thyme
- 1 teaspoon cayenne
- ½ teaspoon fresh-ground black pepper
- 1¼ teaspoons salt
- 1 teaspoon grated nutmeg
- 2 tablespoons brown sugar
- ¼ teaspoon vinegar
- ¼ cup cooking oil
- 4 whole chicken legs

1. In a food processor or blender, puree all the ingredients except the chicken legs. Put the chicken in a large roasting pan and coat with the pureed mixture. Let the chicken marinate for about 30 minutes.

2. Heat the oven to 450°. Cook the chicken legs in the upper third of the oven for 15 minutes. Turn the legs over and cook until just done, about 15 minutes longer.

MENU SUGGESTIONS

Corn bread, rice and beans (or just plain rice), or corn on the cob would all taste great with this highly spiced chicken. Fried plantains are another appropriate accompaniment.

TEST-KITCHEN TIP

The longer you can marinate the chicken legs, the more the flavor will penetrate the meat. We've suggested thirty minutes, but you can marinate the chicken for up to twenty-four hours.

BAKED BUFFALO CHICKEN WINGS

Most of us think of Buffalo wings as bar food, but with their accompaniment of celery sticks and creamy blue-cheese dressing, they make a fine casual meal. These wings are hot, but if you like them incendiary, pass extra Tabasco at the table.

WINE RECOMMENDATION
Beer is a no-brainer with the salt, spice, and heat of this barfly classic. For a more festive alternative, serve a crisp sparkling wine; it will refresh the palate and tame the heat of the dish.

SERVES 4

    4   pounds chicken wings
    3   tablespoons cooking oil
    4   cloves garlic, chopped
 1³⁄₄   teaspoons salt
 1¹⁄₂   teaspoons cayenne
  ²⁄₃   cup mayonnaise
  ¹⁄₃   cup sour cream
  ¹⁄₄   pound blue cheese, crumbled
        (about 1 cup)
    2   scallions including green tops, chopped
    5   teaspoons vinegar
  ¹⁄₄   teaspoon fresh-ground black pepper
  ¹⁄₄   cup ketchup
    1   tablespoon Tabasco sauce
    8   ribs celery, cut into sticks

1. Heat the oven to 425°. In a large bowl, combine the wings, oil, garlic, 1¹⁄₂ teaspoons of the salt, and the cayenne. Arrange the wings in a single layer on two large baking sheets. Bake until just done, about 25 minutes.

2. Meanwhile, in a medium glass or stainless-steel bowl, combine the mayonnaise, sour cream, blue cheese, scallions, 1 teaspoon of the vinegar, the remaining ¹⁄₄ teaspoon salt, and the black pepper.

3. In a large bowl, combine the ketchup, the remaining 4 teaspoons vinegar, and the Tabasco sauce. Add the wings and toss to coat. Serve the wings with the celery sticks and blue-cheese dressing alongside.

MENU SUGGESTIONS

Pair these wings with more finger food. Corn on the cob would go nicely. Roasted potato wedges are a good alternative and can be cooked alongside the wings.

CHICKEN WITH LEMON, OREGANO, AND FETA CHEESE

A trio of Greek flavors gives these chicken quarters Mediterranean flair. The cheese is sprinkled over the cooked chicken, which is then broiled until golden.

WINE RECOMMENDATION

This Greek-flavored dish will go nicely with a number of rustic, spicy red wines. Try finding a bottle from the Greek island of Paros or Santorini. Another alternative would be a syrah-based wine such as a Crozes-Hermitage from the northern Rhône Valley in France.

SERVES 4

1   chicken (3 to 3½ pounds), quartered

1   tablespoon olive oil

1½ teaspoons dried oregano

1   tablespoon lemon juice

¼   teaspoon salt

⅛   teaspoon fresh-ground black pepper

1   tablespoon butter, cut into 4 pieces

1½ ounces feta cheese, crumbled (about ⅓ cup)

1. Heat the oven to 375°. Coat the chicken with the oil; arrange the pieces, skin-side up, in a large roasting pan. Sprinkle the chicken with the oregano, lemon juice, salt, and pepper. Top each piece of chicken with a piece of the butter.

2. Cook the chicken until the breasts are just done, about 30 minutes. Remove the breasts and continue to cook the legs until done, about 5 minutes longer. Remove the roasting pan from the oven; return the breasts to the pan. Top the chicken pieces with the feta cheese. Press any cheese that rolls off into the pan back onto the chicken. Baste the chicken with the pan juices.

3. Heat the broiler. Broil the chicken until golden brown, about 2 minutes. Serve with the pan juices.

MENU SUGGESTIONS

Balance the tanginess of lemon and feta with a mild side dish such as orzo tossed with a little olive oil or sautéed zucchini.

CHICKEN BREASTS WITH CREAMY VEGETABLE TOPPING

Red bell pepper, scallion, and carrot are sautéed briefly, then mixed with cream cheese to form a bright, speckled sauce that bakes right on the chicken—simple and delicious.

WINE RECOMMENDATION
A crisp and fruity white will cut through the rich cheese and pair well with the acidity of the bell pepper and scallion. A kabinett riesling from the Mosel-Saar-Ruwer region of Germany or, if you can find it, a riesling from the Finger Lakes in New York is a good possibility.

SERVES 4

- 1 tablespoon cooking oil
- 1 red bell pepper, chopped
- 2 scallions including green tops, chopped
- 1 carrot, grated
- 8 ounces cream cheese, at room temperature
- 1 teaspoon salt
- ½ teaspoon fresh-ground black pepper
- 4 bone-in chicken breasts (about 2¼ pounds in all), skin removed

1. Heat the oven to 425°. In a medium frying pan, heat the oil over moderate heat. Add the bell pepper and cook, stirring occasionally, until starting to soften, about 3 minutes. Add the scallions and carrot and cook 2 minutes longer. Mix the vegetables with the cream cheese, ¾ teaspoon of the salt, and ¼ teaspoon of the black pepper.

2. Sprinkle the chicken breasts with the remaining ¼ teaspoons of salt and pepper. Put the breasts in a roasting pan and spread them with the vegetable cream cheese. Bake the chicken until just done, 20 to 25 minutes.

MENU SUGGESTIONS

The rich topping on the chicken leaves one wanting a simply prepared vegetable, such as steamed broccoli, asparagus, or green beans.

VARIATION

CHICKEN BREASTS WITH BOURSIN-CHEESE SAUCE

Substitute a 5½-ounce package of plain or garlic-and-herb-flavored Boursin cheese for the cream cheese.

CHICKEN AND EGGPLANT PARMESAN

In this delicious new take on classic eggplant Parmesan, broiled eggplant is layered with fresh mozzarella, basil, and slices of chicken. If basil isn't in season, don't turn to dried basil; it has little flavor. Substitute one teaspoon dried marjoram instead, adding it to the tomato sauce with the salt.

WINE RECOMMENDATION

An Italian red wine such as a reasonably priced nebbiolo from either the Piedmont or Lombardy region has plenty of acidity and body to stand up to the rich taste of this dish.

SERVES 4

- 1 small eggplant (about 1 pound), cut into ¼-inch rounds
- 4 tablespoons olive oil
- 1 teaspoon salt
  Fresh-ground black pepper
- 1 pound boneless, skinless chicken breasts (about 3)
- 2 cups canned crushed tomatoes in thick puree
- ½ pound fresh mozzarella, cut into thin slices
- ⅓ cup grated Parmesan cheese
- ¼ cup lightly packed basil leaves

1. Heat the broiler. Arrange the eggplant in a single layer on a large baking sheet. Coat both sides of the eggplant with 2½ tablespoons of the oil and sprinkle with ½ teaspoon of the salt and ¼ teaspoon pepper. Broil, turning once, until browned, about 5 minutes per side. Turn off the broiler and heat the oven to 425°.

2. In a large nonstick frying pan, heat 1 tablespoon of the oil over moderately high heat. Season the chicken with ¼ teaspoon of the salt and ⅛ teaspoon pepper and add to the pan. Partially cook the chicken for 2 minutes per side and remove from the pan. When cool enough to handle, cut the chicken crosswise into ¼-inch slices.

3. Oil an 8-inch square baking dish. Put one third of the eggplant in a single layer in the dish. Top with half of the chicken, half of the tomatoes, half of the mozzarella, one third of the Parmesan, half of the basil, and the remaining ¼ teaspoon of salt. Repeat with another third of the eggplant, the remaining chicken, tomatoes, and mozzarella, another third of the Parmesan, and the remaining basil. Top with the remaining eggplant and sprinkle with the remaining cheese. Drizzle with the remaining ½ tablespoon oil. Bake for 20 minutes and let sit for 5 minutes before cutting.

CHICKEN AND BRUSSELS SPROUTS OVER WHITE-BEAN AND ROSEMARY PUREE

A drizzle of pan juices ties everything together to make a complete meal that's welcome during the winter. Cannellini, one of our favorite canned beans, make a quick, delicious puree.

WINE RECOMMENDATION
Pair this Mediterranean-inspired dish with a full-flavored red from France. Try one from the southern Rhône Valley such as a Châteauneuf-du-Pape or a Côtes-du-Rhône.

SERVES 4

¾ pound Brussels sprouts, cut in half from top to stem

4 tablespoons olive oil

Salt

Fresh-ground black pepper

4 chicken thighs

4 chicken drumsticks

2 cloves garlic, minced

1 teaspoon dried rosemary, crumbled, or 1 tablespoon chopped fresh rosemary

4 cups drained and rinsed white beans, preferably cannellini (from two 19-ounce cans)

½ cup water

2 tablespoons chopped flat-leaf parsley

1. Heat the oven to 450°. In a medium bowl, toss the Brussels sprouts with 1 tablespoon of the oil, ¼ teaspoon of salt, and ¼ of teaspoon pepper. Set aside.

2. Put the chicken pieces in a large roasting pan and toss with 1 tablespoon of oil, ¼ teaspoon salt, and ¼ teaspoon pepper. Arrange the chicken pieces about 1 inch apart, skin-side up, and roast for 25 minutes. Add the Brussels sprouts and continue cooking until the chicken and sprouts are done, about 12 minutes longer. Transfer them to a plate and leave to rest in a warm spot for about 5 minutes.

3. Meanwhile, in a medium saucepan, heat the remaining 2 tablespoons oil, the garlic, and the rosemary over low heat, stirring, for 3 minutes. Raise the heat to moderate and add the beans, ¼ cup of the water, ¼ teaspoon salt, and ⅛ teaspoon pepper. Cook, mashing the beans to a coarse puree, until hot, about 5 minutes. Stir in the parsley.

4. Pour off the fat from the roasting pan. Set the pan over moderate heat and add the remaining ¼ cup water. Bring to a boil, scraping the bottom of the pan to dislodge any brown bits. Boil until reduced to ¼ cup, about 4 minutes. Add any accumulated juices from the chicken and a pinch each of salt and pepper. Spoon the white-bean puree onto plates and top with the chicken, the Brussels sprouts, and then the pan juices.

CORNISH HENS WITH SCALLION BUTTER AND LIME

The typical Mexican combination of cumin and lime works beautifully with Cornish hens. Scallion butter both moistens the cooked birds and adds an extra fillip of flavor.

WINE RECOMMENDATION
A number of hearty red wines would be nice with the straightforward, rustic flavors here. Look for a Corbières from the south of France, a zinfandel from California, or a Rosso di Montalcino from Tuscany in Italy.

SERVES 4

- 4 tablespoons butter, at room temperature
- 1 teaspoon dried oregano
- 1 teaspoon cumin
- 1/2 teaspoon salt
  Fresh-ground black pepper
- 2 Cornish hens (about 1 1/4 pounds each), halved
- 1 scallion including green top, chopped
  Lime wedges, for serving

1. Heat the oven to 450°. In a small bowl, combine 2 tablespoons of the butter with the oregano, cumin, 1/4 teaspoon of the salt, and 1/4 teaspoon pepper.

2. Rub the mixture over the skin of the hens and arrange them, skin-side up, on a baking sheet. Roast in the upper third of the oven until golden and cooked through, about 20 minutes.

3. Meanwhile, combine the remaining 2 tablespoons butter with the scallion, the remaining 1/4 teaspoon salt, and 1/8 teaspoon pepper. When the hens are roasted, top with the scallion butter. Serve with lime wedges.

MENU SUGGESTIONS

You could roast new potatoes right alongside the hens with almost no effort. Sautéed bell peppers would complete the meal.

VARIATION

CORNISH HENS WITH HERB BUTTER AND LIME

Mix one tablespoon chopped fresh herbs, such as chives, parsley, and/or oregano, with the butter in place of the scallions.

CORNISH HENS WITH FRUIT, WALNUTS, AND HONEY APPLE GLAZE

Dried fruits, fresh apples, and nuts make a delightful dressing for these roasted Cornish hens. The dish seems perfect for a chilly fall evening, but it can certainly be served any time of the year.

WINE RECOMMENDATION
The fruits and nuts in this dish will pair well with the rich texture and flavor of a Tokay Pinot Gris, a white from Alsace in France. A red wine with plenty of fruit flavor, such as a grenache from California, would be another good match.

SERVES 4

2 tart apples, such as Granny Smith, peeled, cored, and diced

2/3 cup dried apricots, cut into thin slices

2/3 cup raisins

1 cup walnuts, chopped

1/4 teaspoon cinnamon

2 tablespoons melted butter

1/4 cup apple juice

2 tablespoons honey

1/4 teaspoon dried thyme

1/2 teaspoon salt

2 Cornish hens (about 1 1/4 pounds each), halved

1/4 teaspoon fresh-ground black pepper

1. Heat the oven to 425°. In a roasting pan, combine the apples, apricots, raisins, walnuts, cinnamon, and butter. Spread the mixture over the bottom of the pan.

2. In a small bowl, combine the apple juice, honey, thyme, and 1/4 teaspoon of the salt to make a glaze. Sprinkle the Cornish hens with the remaining 1/4 teaspoon salt and the pepper and set them breast-side down on top of the fruit-and-nut mixture. Brush the hens with some of the glaze and then cook for 10 minutes.

3. Remove the roasting pan from the oven. Stir the fruit-and-nut mixture and turn the hens over. Brush them with more of the glaze, return the pan to the oven, and cook until just done, about 15 minutes longer. Glaze the hens one final time and serve them with the fruit-and-nut dressing.

MENU SUGGESTIONS

Earthy wild rice or bulgar pilaf will balance the sweet fruit dressing here.

GRILLED CHICKEN BREASTS WITH GRAPEFRUIT GLAZE

Simply prepared yet special, these chicken breasts are grilled and basted with a bitter, tart, and sweet glaze.

WINE RECOMMENDATION
The crisp acidity, effervescence, and moderate alcohol level of a brut Champagne from France or a sparkling wine from California will be perfect with the smokey taste here and with the high acidity of the grapefruit juice.

SERVES 4

2   cloves garlic, minced

1   teaspoon grapefruit zest (from about ½ grapefruit)

½   cup grapefruit juice (from 1 grapefruit)

1   tablespoon cooking oil

2   tablespoons honey

½   teaspoon salt

¼   teaspoon fresh-ground black pepper

4   bone-in chicken breasts (about 2¼ pounds in all)

1. Light the grill. In a small bowl, combine the garlic, grapefruit zest, grapefruit juice, oil, honey, salt, and pepper.

2. Grill the chicken breasts over moderately high heat, brushing frequently with the glaze, for 8 minutes. Turn and cook, brushing with more glaze, until the chicken is just done, 10 to 12 minutes longer. Remove.

3. In a small stainless-steel saucepan, bring the remaining glaze to a boil. Boil for about 1 minute, remove from the heat, and pour over the grilled chicken.

MENU SUGGESTIONS

Since the chicken breasts don't have a lot of sauce, serve a juicy vegetable such as grilled or sautéed summer squash or zucchini alongside.

VARIATION

GRILLED CHICKEN BREASTS WITH CITRUS GLAZE

Use a combination of citrus juices, such as orange, lemon, or lime, instead of all or part of the grapefruit juice.

GRILLED CHICKEN WITH SPICY BRAZILIAN TOMATO AND COCONUT SAUCE

Redolent of ginger and jalapeños, the tomato sauce is a lively addition to plain grilled chicken. If you like less heat, use only one jalapeño.

WINE RECOMMENDATION
This spicy dish will demolish any subtlety in a wine. Go for something straightforward and gulpable: a fresh white wine such as a pinot bianco from northern Italy, a slightly chilled red such as Beaujolais from France, or a beer.

SERVES 4

- 4 tablespoons cooking oil
- 3 cloves garlic, minced
- 1 chicken (3 to 3½ pounds), quartered
- ¾ teaspoon salt
  Fresh-ground black pepper
- 1 onion, chopped
- 1 tablespoon minced fresh ginger
- 2 jalapeño peppers, seeds and ribs removed, minced
- 1¼ cups canned crushed tomatoes in thick puree
- 1 cup canned unsweetened coconut milk
- 2 tablespoons chopped cilantro or parsley

1. Light the grill. In a shallow dish, combine 3 tablespoons of the oil with two-thirds of the minced garlic. Coat the chicken with half of the garlic oil and season with ¼ teaspoon of the salt and ⅛ teaspoon pepper. Grill the chicken over moderately high heat, basting with the remaining garlic oil, until just done, about 10 minutes per side for the breasts, 13 for the legs.

2. Meanwhile, in a medium saucepan, heat the remaining 1 tablespoon oil over moderately low heat. Add the onion and cook, stirring occasionally, until translucent, about 5 minutes. Add the remaining garlic, the ginger, and the jalapeños, and cook, stirring, for 1 minute longer. Add the tomatoes, the coconut milk, the remaining ½ teaspoon salt, and a pinch of pepper. Bring to a simmer and cook, stirring occasionally, until thickened, about 5 minutes. Stir in the cilantro and serve with the chicken.

MENU SUGGESTIONS

Rice and beans or refried beans are typical Brazilian side dishes that taste especially good with chicken.

GRILLED TANDOORI CHICKEN

Flavored by a yogurt and spice paste with ginger, cumin, and coriander, this chicken tastes almost as good as if it were cooked in a tandoor oven. Like Indian cooks, we remove the chicken skin and score the flesh so that the spice paste penetrates.

WINE RECOMMENDATION
Spicy dishes such as this pair best with wines with low alcohol, high acidity, and a touch of fruitiness. Try an off-dry riesling from Oregon, California, or New York State.

SERVES 4

- 1 chicken (3 to 3½ pounds), cut into 8 pieces and skin removed
- 3 tablespoons lemon juice
- 1½ tablespoons water
- 1½ teaspoons salt
- ¼ teaspoon ground turmeric
- ½ cup plain yogurt
- 2 large garlic cloves, chopped
- 1 tablespoon chopped fresh ginger
- 1¼ teaspoons ground coriander
- ¾ teaspoon ground cumin
- ⅛ teaspoon cayenne
- 3 tablespoons cooking oil

1. Light the grill. Using a sharp knife, cut shallow incisions in the chicken pieces at about ½-inch intervals. In a large, glass dish or stainless-steel pan, combine the lemon juice, water, salt, and turmeric. Add the chicken pieces and turn to coat. Let the chicken pieces marinate for 5 minutes.

2. Meanwhile, in a small bowl, combine the yogurt, garlic, ginger, coriander, cumin, and cayenne. Add to the chicken and lemon mixture; turn to coat. Let marinate for 10 minutes.

3. Grill the chicken over moderately high heat, basting with oil, for 10 minutes. Turn and cook, basting with the remaining oil, until just done, about 10 minutes longer for the breasts, 12 for the thighs and drumsticks.

MENU SUGGESTIONS

Indian flatbread, such as naan, is the traditional accompaniment to tandoori. You can grill store-bought naan or other flatbread, such as pita or lavash. In summer, the sweetness of grilled corn on the cob makes a nice balance to the spiciness of the chicken. Another option is eggplant, a favorite vegetable in India, sliced and grilled.

GRILLED CORNISH HENS WITH SUN-DRIED-TOMATO PESTO

Since the tomato pesto here is made in a processor or blender, you have to make more than the small quantity needed. Use leftover pesto later in the week on grilled vegetables or fish. It's also a delicious addition to sandwiches, not to mention pasta.

WINE RECOMMENDATION
For this grilled dish, with its smoke, salt, and acidity (from tomatoes), choose a wine that's simple and refreshing. Among the many options are Italian red wines with good acidity such as Chianti Classico or dolcetto.

SERVES 4

2/3 cup reconstituted sun-dried tomatoes, or sun-dried tomatoes packed in oil, drained

2 cloves garlic, chopped

3 tablespoons grated Parmesan cheese

3/4 teaspoon salt

1/4 teaspoon fresh-ground black pepper

1 tablespoon lemon juice

1/2 cup olive oil

2 Cornish hens (about 1 1/4 pounds each), halved

1. Light the grill. In a food processor or blender, mince the tomatoes and garlic with the Parmesan, salt, pepper, and lemon juice. With the machine running, add the oil in a thin stream and continue whirring until the ingredients are well mixed.

2. With your fingers, loosen the skin from the breast meat of each hen, leaving the skin around the edge attached. For each half hen, spread 1 tablespoon of pesto under the skin and 1 tablespoon over it. Cook the hens over moderate heat, skin-side down, for 12 minutes. Turn the hens and cook until just done, about 12 minutes longer.

MENU SUGGESTIONS

Creamy polenta topped with a dollop of the extra pesto will be perfect with the hens. Also, since the grill is already hot, you might throw on some vegetables—peppers, zucchini, asparagus.

RECONSTITUTING SUN-DRIED TOMATOES

In a small pan, bring enough water to a boil to cover the dried tomatoes. Add the tomatoes, then remove from the heat and let them steep in the hot water for about 5 minutes. Drain.

GRILLED CORNISH HENS WITH RICE AND SICILIAN BUTTER

The traditional combination of olives, anchovies, and oranges shows up here in a flavored butter that adds a special richness and intensity to hens hot off the grill. Make a double batch and keep the extra in your freezer to use at a moment's notice.

WINE RECOMMENDATION
The saltiness of olives and anchovies can make the wrong wine appear coarse and too alcoholic. A rosé is the perfect choice. If you can find one from Sicily, buy it. If not, pick a bottle from Navarre in Spain or from the south of France.

SERVES 4

8 tablespoons butter, at room temperature

1/3 cup black olives, such as Kalamata, halved and pitted

2 teaspoons anchovy paste

1 tablespoon grated orange zest (from about 1 navel orange)

2 teaspoons orange juice

2 cloves garlic, minced

1/4 teaspoon fresh-ground black pepper

2 Cornish hens (about 1¼ pounds each), halved

2 tablespoons cooking oil

Boiled or steamed rice, for serving

1. Light the grill. In a food processor, puree the butter and olives with the anchovy paste, orange zest, orange juice, garlic, and pepper.

With a rubber spatula, scrape the butter into a small bowl and refrigerate.

2. Rub the hens with oil and cook over moderate heat for 12 minutes. Turn and cook until just done, about 12 minutes longer.

3. Remove the hens from the grill and serve with the rice. Top each serving with 2 tablespoons of the flavored butter, letting the butter melt over both the hen and the rice.

MENU SUGGESTIONS

You might grill some eggplant slices and drizzle them with balsamic vinegar to go with these hens. Sautéed broccoli rabe with garlic and a sprinkling of Parmesan would also match the Italian mood.

GRILLED ASIAN CORNISH HENS WITH ASPARAGUS AND PORTOBELLO MUSHROOMS

Though marinated only briefly with lime juice, garlic, ginger, and soy sauce, the Cornish hens and vegetables nevertheless have a deliciously intense flavor.

WINE RECOMMENDATION
An acidic, assertively flavored white wine, such as a sauvignon blanc from Australia or South Africa, is great with the asparagus and the bold flavors of the soy sauce and lime juice.

SERVES 4

6	tablespoons soy sauce
¼	cup lime juice (from about 2 limes)
¼	cup cooking oil
4	cloves garlic, minced
1	teaspoon ground ginger
½	teaspoon fresh-ground black pepper
¼	teaspoon salt
2	Cornish hens (about 1¼ pounds each), halved
1	pound asparagus
⅔	pound portobello mushrooms, stems removed, caps cut into ¼-inch slices, or 6 ounces sliced portobello mushrooms

1. Light the grill. In a small glass or stainless-steel bowl, combine the soy sauce, lime juice, oil, garlic, ginger, pepper, and salt. Put the hens into two large glass dishes. Pour ½ cup of the marinade over them and turn to coat. Let marinate, turning once, for 10 minutes.

2. Cook the hens over moderate heat for 12 minutes. Turn and cook until just done, about 12 minutes longer.

3. Meanwhile, snap off and discard the tough ends of the asparagus. In a medium bowl, toss the asparagus spears with 2 tablespoons of the remaining marinade and grill for about 12 minutes, turning once.

4. In the same bowl, toss the mushrooms with the remaining 2 tablespoons marinade and grill for about 5 minutes per side. Serve the hens with the asparagus and mushrooms alongside.

MENU SUGGESTIONS

Make your whole dinner outdoors by adding new potatoes or sweet-potato wedges to the grill.

CHAPTER THREE

Soups, Stews, Curries & Other Braised Dishes

THAI CHICKEN AND COCONUT SOUP WITH NOODLES

With its seductive flavors of coconut, lime, ginger, and cilantro, this Thai soup is quickly becoming a favorite across the country. Our version includes enough chicken and noodles to make it a main course. If you like, turn up the heat with more cayenne.

WINE RECOMMENDATION
The spices and the coconut milk will be best accompanied by a wine with a hint of sweetness. Try a chenin blanc from California or a demi-sec version of Vouvray (also made from the chenin blanc grape).

SERVES 4

1½ tablespoons cooking oil
1 small onion, chopped
4 cloves garlic, minced
1½ teaspoons ground coriander
½ teaspoon ground ginger
¼ teaspoon fresh-ground black pepper
⅛ teaspoon cayenne
1 quart canned low-sodium chicken broth or homemade stock
2 cups canned unsweetened coconut milk
5 teaspoons Asian fish sauce (nam pla or nuoc mam)* or soy sauce
1¾ teaspoons salt
2 3-inch-long strips lime zest
½ pound egg fettuccine
1 pound boneless, skinless chicken breasts (about 3), cut into ¼-inch slices

2 tablespoons lime juice
3 tablespoons chopped cilantro (optional)

*Available at Asian markets and some supermarkets

1. In a large pot, heat the cooking oil over moderately low heat. Add the onion and cook, stirring occasionally, until it is translucent, about 5 minutes. Add the garlic, coriander, ginger, black pepper, and cayenne; cook, stirring, for 30 seconds.

2. Add the broth, coconut milk, fish sauce, salt, and lime zest. Bring to a simmer, stirring occasionally. Reduce the heat and simmer, partially covered, for 10 minutes.

3. Meanwhile, in a large pot of boiling, salted water, cook the fettuccine until just done, about 12 minutes. Drain.

4. Add the chicken to the soup and simmer until just done, about 1½ minutes. Remove the pot from the heat and stir in the fettuccine, lime juice, and cilantro, if using. Serve the soup in bowls with a fork and spoon.

KALE AND POTATO SOUP WITH TURKEY SAUSAGE

The traditional Portuguese kale and potato soup inspired this delicious country-style dish. It's especially welcome in the winter months when kale is at its peak.

WINE RECOMMENDATION
An aromatic, acidic white wine such as a sauvignon blanc is always a great choice for leafy greens. But the heartiness of this country soup can also work well with a full-bodied Portuguese red wine such as a Dão.

SERVES 4

1 tablespoon cooking oil

1 pound turkey or chicken sausage

1 onion, chopped

4 cloves garlic, cut into thin slices

1 quart water

2 cups canned low-sodium chicken broth or homemade stock

1½ teaspoons salt

1½ pounds boiling potatoes, peeled and cut into ¼-inch pieces

Pinch dried red-pepper flakes

1 pound kale, stems removed, leaves shredded

¼ teaspoon fresh-ground black pepper

1. In a large pot, heat the oil over moderately low heat. Add the sausage and cook, turning, until browned, about 10 minutes. Remove the sausage from the pot and, when it is cool enough to handle, cut it into slices. Pour off all but 1 tablespoon fat from the pan.

2. Add the onion and cook, stirring occasionally, until it is translucent, about 5 minutes. Add the garlic to the pan and cook, stirring, for 1 minute longer.

3. Add the water, broth, and salt and bring the soup to a boil. Add the sausage, potatoes, and red-pepper flakes and bring back to a simmer. Cook, partially covered, for 2 minutes. Add the kale and bring the soup back to a simmer. Cook, partially covered, until the potatoes and kale are tender, about 6 minutes longer. Add the black pepper.

MENU SUGGESTIONS

An interesting bread completes this meal with aplomb. Try corn bread or tomato-topped Italian focaccia. A good crusty loaf of white bread will do fine, too.

SPICY CHICKEN CHILI

Serving this spicy stew is a surefire way to please everyone at the table. Leftover turkey or chicken can be substituted for the chicken thighs.

WINE RECOMMENDATION
A red wine with plenty of acidity is best suited to the spice and heat here. Look for a sangiovese from California or a dolcetto from the Piedmont region of Italy.

SERVES 4

- 2 tablespoons cooking oil
- 1 onion, chopped
- 2 cloves garlic, minced
- 1 pound skinless chicken thighs (about 4), cut into thin strips
- 4 teaspoons chili powder
- 1 tablespoon ground cumin
- 2 teaspoons dried oregano
- 1 teaspoon salt
- 2 jalapeño peppers, seeds and ribs removed, chopped
- 1½ cups canned crushed tomatoes with their juice
- 2½ cups canned low-sodium chicken broth or homemade stock
- 1⅔ cups drained and rinsed pinto beans (from one 15-ounce can)
- 1⅔ cups drained and rinsed black beans (from one 15-ounce can)
- ½ teaspoon fresh-ground black pepper
- ⅓ cup chopped cilantro (optional)

1. In a large saucepan, heat the oil over moderately low heat. Add the onion and garlic; cook until they start to soften, about 3 minutes.

2. Increase the heat to moderate and stir in the chicken strips. Cook until they are no longer pink, about 2 minutes. Stir in the chili powder, cumin, oregano, and salt. Add the jalapeños, the tomatoes with their juice, and the broth. Bring to a boil, reduce the heat, cover, and simmer for 15 minutes.

3. Uncover the saucepan and stir in the beans and black pepper. Simmer until the chili is thickened, about 15 minutes longer. Serve topped with the cilantro.

MENU SUGGESTIONS

Wedges of corn bread are always a good complement to chili. Or serve the chili over macaroni or rice.

GROUNDNUT STEW

Peanut butter and okra flavor and thicken this tasty African stew. You can substitute green beans for the okra, if you like; the consistency of the sauce won't be quite the same, but it will still be thick enough to cling to the chicken.

WINE RECOMMENDATION

A simple, fruity red wine such as a Beaujolais (or, if it's December through March, a Beaujolais Nouveau) will make a lively companion to the peanut butter in this stew.

SERVES 4

2   tablespoons cooking oil, more if needed

1   chicken (3 to 3½ pounds), cut into 8 pieces

1¾ teaspoons salt

½   teaspoon fresh-ground black pepper

1   onion, chopped

2   tablespoons tomato paste

1   cup canned crushed tomatoes, drained

¼   teaspoon cayenne

2¾ cups water

½   cup creamy peanut butter

1   10-ounce package frozen sliced okra

1. In a large pot, heat the oil over moderately high heat. Season the chicken pieces with ¼ teaspoon each of the salt and black pepper. Cook until browned, turning, about 8 minutes in all. Remove. Pour off all but 1 tablespoon fat from the pot.

2   Reduce the heat to moderately low. Add the onion to the pot and cook, stirring occasionally, until starting to soften, about 3 minutes. Stir in the tomato paste and then the tomatoes and cayenne. Return the chicken legs and thighs to the pot and stir in 2 cups of the water. Bring to a simmer and cook, partially covered, for 10 minutes.

3. Whisk together the peanut butter and the remaining ¾ cup water until smooth. Add this mixture to the stew along with the chicken breasts and wings, the okra and the remaining 1½ teaspoons of salt and ¼ teaspoon of black pepper. Cook, partially covered, until the okra is just done, about 10 minutes.

MENU SUGGESTIONS

Serve the stew with rice or egg noodles to capture every drop of the distinctive sauce.

CHICKEN STEW WITH CIDER AND PARSNIPS

Carrots, parsnips, and chicken simmer in a sauce of apple cider and chicken broth, making a delicious and homey stew—perfect for a chilly fall evening.

WINE RECOMMENDATION
A "comfort" wine will make this dish even more satisfying. A rustic red from the south of France, such as a Cahors or Minervois, is a good possibility.

SERVES 4

- 2 tablespoons cooking oil
- 4 chicken thighs
- 4 chicken drumsticks
- ¾ teaspoon salt
- ¼ teaspoon fresh-ground black pepper
- 1 tablespoon flour
- 1 cup apple cider
- 1½ cups canned low-sodium chicken broth or homemade stock
- 1 onion, cut into thin slices
- 1 pound parsnips, cut into 1-inch pieces
- 2 carrots, cut into 1-inch pieces
- ½ teaspoon dried thyme

1. Heat the oven to 400°. In a large pot or Dutch oven, heat the oil over moderately high heat. Season the chicken thighs and drumsticks with ¼ teaspoon of the salt and the pepper. Cook the chicken until browned, turning, about 8 minutes in all. Remove. Pour off all but 1 tablespoon of the fat from the pot.

2. Reduce the heat to moderate and stir in the flour. Whisk in the cider and the broth and bring to a simmer, scraping the bottom of the pot to dislodge any brown bits. Add the onion, parsnips, carrots, thyme, and the remaining ½ teaspoon of salt. Simmer, partially covered, for 10 minutes.

3. Return the chicken to the pot. Bring the stew back to a simmer, cover, and put in the preheated oven until the chicken is done and the vegetables are tender, about 15 minutes.

MENU SUGGESTIONS

Simple boiled potatoes, egg noodles, or rice would be perfect for catching the stew's extra sauce.

INDIAN-SPICED CHICKEN AND SPINACH

The flavor of this dish is rich, fragrant, and mellow—not hot. You can make the sauce ahead of time and simmer the chicken in it just before serving.

WINE RECOMMENDATION
An off-dry chenin blanc from California or a chenin-blanc-based French Vouvray (look for a demi-sec) will be lovely with the aromatic cream sauce. The acidity of these wines and their melon and apricot notes are perfect foils for the exotic stew.

SERVES 4

2 tablespoons cooking oil

1 onion, chopped

3 cloves garlic, chopped

1 tablespoon chopped fresh ginger

1 tablespoon ground cumin

1 tablespoon ground coriander

½ teaspoon turmeric

½ teaspoon paprika

1½ teaspoons salt

2 jalapeño peppers, seeds and ribs removed, minced

½ cup canned crushed tomatoes, drained

½ cup heavy cream

1 cinnamon stick

1½ cups water

2 10-ounce packages frozen chopped spinach, thawed

4 boneless, skinless chicken breasts (about 1⅓ pounds in all), cut into 3 pieces each

1. In a large frying pan, heat the oil over moderately low heat. Add the onion and cook until starting to soften, about 3 minutes. Add the garlic and ginger and cook, stirring occasionally, for 2 minutes longer. Stir in the cumin, coriander, turmeric, paprika, and 1 teaspoon of the salt. Cook until the spices are fragrant, about 1 minute, and then stir in the jalapeños and tomatoes. Add the cream, cinnamon stick, and water. Squeeze the spinach to remove excess liquid and add the spinach to the pan. Bring to a simmer. Cover the pan, reduce the heat, and simmer for 5 minutes.

2. Stir in the chicken and the remaining ½ teaspoon salt, cover, and simmer the stew until just done, about 10 minutes. Remove the cinnamon stick before serving.

MENU SUGGESTIONS

Indian basmati rice would be an ideal accompaniment here, but plain white rice will work well, too.

MASSAMAN CURRY

So many curries are made throughout the world that it's hard to pick favorites. But this dish, based on a Thai and Muslim combination including potatoes, peanuts, and five-spice powder, must be one of the best.

WINE RECOMMENDATION
For this bold curry, bursting with heat, spice, and sweetness, a fresh, aromatic white that won't get pushed around—a chenin blanc from the Loire Valley in France or from California, for example, or a sauvignon blanc from New Zealand—is a good match.

SERVES 4

1 tablespoon cooking oil

1 onion, chopped

2 cloves garlic, minced

1 teaspoon chopped fresh ginger

1 teaspoon Chinese five-spice powder

1 teaspoon ground cumin

1/4 teaspoon cayenne

1/4 teaspoon turmeric

1 teaspoon salt

1 cup canned low-sodium chicken broth or homemade stock

1/2 cup canned unsweetened coconut milk or heavy cream

1/2 pound boiling potatoes (about 2), peeled and cut into 1/2-inch pieces

1 1/3 pounds boneless, skinless chicken breasts (about 4), cut into 1/2-inch pieces

1/2 cup chopped peanuts

1/2 pound plum tomatoes (about 4), cut into wedges

3 tablespoons chopped cilantro

1. In a large saucepan, heat the oil over moderately low heat. Add the onion and cook, stirring occasionally, until it is translucent, about 5 minutes. Add the garlic, ginger, five-spice powder, cumin, cayenne, turmeric, and 1/2 teaspoon of the salt. Stir until fragrant, about 1 minute. Whisk in the broth and then the coconut milk; bring to a simmer. Stir in the potatoes, cover, and cook over low heat until they are almost tender, about 12 minutes.

2. Add the chicken to the sauce, cover, and simmer for 5 minutes. Stir in the peanuts, tomatoes, cilantro, and the remaining 1/2 teaspoon salt. Turn the heat off, cover, and let steam until the chicken is just done, about 2 minutes longer.

MENU SUGGESTION

For this curry, steamed white rice is the only accompaniment you need.

SPICED CHICKEN LEGS WITH APRICOTS AND RAISINS

Fruity and peppery, this exotic dish will perk up your midweek menu. Yet it's no more trouble than the simplest chicken recipe in your repertoire.

WINE RECOMMENDATION
The sweetness here will be nicely mirrored by an off-dry, aromatic white wine, such as a chenin blanc, riesling, or gewürztraminer from California.

SERVES 4

2	tablespoons cooking oil
4	chicken thighs
4	chicken drumsticks
1¾	teaspoons salt
½	teaspoon fresh-ground black pepper
1	onion, chopped
3	cloves garlic, chopped
1¼	cups canned low-sodium chicken broth or homemade stock
¼	teaspoon allspice
¼	teaspoon red-pepper flakes
⅔	cup dried apricots, quartered
¼	cup dark or golden raisins
¼	cup chopped fresh parsley

1. In a large, deep frying pan, heat the oil over moderately high heat. Season the chicken thighs and drumsticks with ¼ teaspoon each of the salt and pepper. Cook the chicken until browned, turning, about 8 minutes in all. Remove. Pour off all but 1 tablespoon of the fat from the pan.

2. Reduce the heat to moderately low. Add the onion and garlic to the pan; cook, stirring occasionally, until the onion starts to soften, about 3 minutes. Add the broth, the remaining 1½ teaspoons salt and ¼ teaspoon black pepper, the allspice, and the red-pepper flakes. Add the chicken, apricots, and raisins. Bring to a simmer, reduce the heat, and simmer the chicken, partially covered, until just done, about 20 minutes. Serve topped with the parsley.

MENU SUGGESTION

Couscous is a natural with this Moroccan-inspired dish.

RUSTIC GARLIC CHICKEN

Yes, *three* heads of garlic. You don't have to peel the cloves first. They soften during cooking and take on a subtle sweetness. Each person squeezes the garlic out of its skin onto the plate to eat with the chicken.

WINE RECOMMENDATION
This simple Gallic dish will work well with a rustic red wine from the south of France. Look for lesser-known, good-value bottles from Corbières or Minervois, or a more serious, tannic wine from Cahors.

SERVES 4

2   tablespoons cooking oil

1   chicken (about 3 to 3½ pounds), cut into 8 pieces

1   teaspoon salt

¼   teaspoon fresh-ground black pepper

3   heads garlic, cloves separated

2   tablespoons flour

1   cup dry white wine

1   cup canned low-sodium chicken broth or homemade stock

2   tablespoons butter

2   tablespoons chopped fresh parsley

1. Heat the oven to 400°. In a Dutch oven, heat the oil over moderately high heat. Sprinkle the chicken with ½ teaspoon of the salt and the pepper. Cook the chicken until well browned, turning, about 8 minutes in all, and remove from the pot. Reduce the heat to moderate, add the garlic, and sauté until it is starting to brown, about 3 minutes. Sprinkle the flour over the garlic and stir until combined. Return the chicken to the pot, cover, and bake for 15 minutes.

2. Remove the pot from the oven and put it on a burner. Remove the chicken pieces from the pot. Over moderately high heat, whisk in the wine and simmer for 1 minute. Whisk in the broth and the remaining ½ teaspoon salt and simmer until starting to thicken, about 3 minutes. Turn the heat off, whisk in the butter, and pour the sauce over the chicken. Sprinkle with the parsley.

MENU SUGGESTIONS

There's plenty of luscious, garlicky sauce here. Take advantage of it with mashed potatoes, egg noodles, or rice.

CHICKEN GOULASH

Fragrant with paprika and brimming with flavor, this Hungarian classic continues to please. Our quick version loses none of the original appeal.

WINE RECOMMENDATION
With this dish, it's natural to experiment with one of the increasing number of reds imported from Hungary. Try Egri Bikavér or a varietal such as a merlot or a cabernet sauvignon.

SERVES 4

1   tablespoon cooking oil

8   chicken thighs

1½   teaspoons salt

1   onion, chopped

2   carrots, cut into ¼-inch slices

2   ribs celery, cut into ¼-inch slices

2   cloves garlic, minced

2   tablespoons paprika

1   tablespoon flour

⅛   teaspoon cayenne

1½   cups canned low-sodium chicken broth or homemade stock

1½   cups canned crushed tomatoes in thick puree

¼   teaspoon dried thyme

1   bay leaf

2   tablespoons chopped fresh parsley

¼   teaspoon fresh-ground black pepper

1. In a large, heavy pot, heat the oil over moderately high heat. Season the chicken with ¼ teaspoon of the salt and add it to the pan. Cook the chicken until browned, turning, about 8 minutes in all. Remove. Pour off all but 1 tablespoon fat from the pan.

2. Add the onion, carrots, celery, and garlic to the pan. Reduce the heat to moderate and cook, stirring occasionally, until the onion is translucent, about 5 minutes.

3. Reduce the heat to moderately low and add the paprika, flour, and cayenne to the pan. Cook, stirring, for 30 seconds. Stir in the broth, tomatoes, the remaining 1¼ teaspoons salt, the thyme, and the bay leaf. Add the chicken and bring to a simmer. Reduce the heat and simmer, partially covered, until the chicken is done, about 20 minutes. Remove the bay leaf and add the parsley and black pepper.

MENU SUGGESTIONS

Serve the goulash with spaetzle, buttered noodles, or boiled or mashed potatoes.

CHICKEN AND CAVATELLI

So comforting and yummy, this dish reminds us of Grandma's chicken and dumplings.
In fact, you can substitute frozen dumplings for the cavatelli.

WINE RECOMMENDATION
Because this dish has no bold or assertive flavors to compete with the wine, options are unlimited: red or white, full-flavored or light-bodied. Three good choices would be a merlot or a chardonnay from California or a Meursault (also made from chardonnay) from France.

SERVES 4

5	cups canned low-sodium chicken broth or homemade stock
1	bay leaf
1	onion, cut into thin slices
2	ribs celery, cut into 1/2-inch pieces
3	carrots, cut into 1/2-inch pieces
1	teaspoon dried sage
1 1/2	teaspoons salt
1/4	teaspoon fresh-ground black pepper
4	bone-in chicken breasts (about 2 1/4 pounds in all)
3/4	pound frozen cavatelli, egg noodles, or dumplings
2	tablespoons butter, softened
2	tablespoons flour

1. In a large pot, bring the broth, bay leaf, onion, celery, and carrots to a simmer. Simmer for 5 minutes. Add the sage, salt, pepper, and chicken breasts and simmer, partially covered, until just done, about 25 minutes. Turn the chicken breasts a few times during cooking.

2. Meanwhile, in a large pot of boiling, salted water, cook the cavatelli until just done, about 10 minutes. Drain.

3. In a small bowl, stir the butter and flour together to form a paste. Remove the bay leaf from the pot, push the chicken to the side and then whisk the butter mixture into the liquid. Simmer until thickened, 1 to 2 minutes. Stir in the cooked cavatelli and simmer until just heated through.

FROZEN PASTA

Several brands of frozen cavatelli, flat egg noodles, and gnocchi are available in supermarkets. Unlike dried pasta, these products have an appealing doughy chew that we find just right with this type of saucy stew. Cook the frozen pasta separately according to package directions, drain, and then stir into the pot with the chicken.

CHICKEN THIGHS WITH LENTILS, CHORIZO, AND RED PEPPER

Reminiscent of cassoulet—the glorious goose, sausage, and bean casserole from southwestern France—this dish is quicker, easier, and bound to become a winter favorite. If you like, use a green bell pepper in place of the red.

WINE RECOMMENDATION

The chorizo, pepper, and lentils pair well with a full-flavored, bold red wine. Two possibilities from France: a red from the Médoc, in Bordeaux, or a Châteauneuf-du-Pape from the southern Rhône Valley.

SERVES 4

1²/₃ cups lentils (about ²/₃ pound)

3 cups water

1 teaspoon salt

¼ teaspoon dried thyme

1 bay leaf

2 tablespoons cooking oil

½ pound dried chorizo or salami, casings removed, cut into ⅛-inch slices

1 onion, chopped

2 cloves garlic, minced

1 red bell pepper, cut into 1-inch pieces

4 chicken thighs

¼ teaspoon fresh-ground black pepper

²/₃ cup canned low-sodium chicken broth or homemade stock

2 tablespoons lemon juice

2 tablespoons chopped fresh parsley

1. In a large saucepan, bring the lentils, water, ¾ teaspoon of the salt, the thyme, and bay leaf to a boil over moderately high heat. Reduce the heat. Simmer, covered, until the lentils are tender but not falling apart, about 25 minutes.

2. Meanwhile, in a large frying pan, heat 1 tablespoon of the oil over moderate heat. Add the chorizo and cook, stirring occasionally, until browned, about 5 minutes. Pour off all but 2 tablespoons of the fat from the pan. Reduce the heat to moderately low and add the onion, garlic, and bell pepper. Cook, stirring occasionally, until the onion is translucent, about 5 minutes. Add the onion mixture to the simmering lentils.

3. Heat the remaining tablespoon of oil in the pan over moderate heat. Season the chicken with the remaining ¼ teaspoon salt and the black pepper and add it to the pan. Cook the chicken, turning, until brown, about 12 minutes in all. Pour off all the fat from the pan. Add the broth, reduce the heat and simmer, covered, until the chicken is just done, about 15 minutes. Add the pan juices from the chicken to the lentils along with the lemon juice and the parsley. Top with the chicken and let sit, covered, for 5 minutes.

CHAPTER FOUR

Pasta
&
Grains

CHICKEN BREASTS WITH ORZO, CARROTS, DILL, AND AVGOLEMONO SAUCE

Avgolemono sauce, a Greek contribution to the world's cuisine, is a delicate blend of chicken broth, dill, and lemon, thickened lightly with egg. In the spring, asparagus would substitute beautifully for the carrots.

WINE RECOMMENDATION
Lemon and dill will work best with a full-flavored white wine with decent acidity. Try one from the southern part of Burgundy such as a Mâcon or Pouilly-Fuissé (both made from chardonnay grapes).

SERVES 4

2 tablespoons olive oil

4 boneless, skinless chicken breasts (about 1 1/3 pounds in all)

Salt and fresh-ground black pepper

1 1/4 cups canned low-sodium chicken broth or homemade stock

1 teaspoon dried dill

1 1/2 cups orzo

4 carrots, quartered and cut into 2-inch lengths

2 eggs

2 tablespoons lemon juice

1. In a large stainless-steel frying pan, heat 1 tablespoon of oil over moderate heat. Season the chicken breasts with 1/4 teaspoon salt and 1/8 teaspoon pepper and add to the pan. Cook until browned, about 5 minutes. Turn the chicken; add the broth, dill, and 1 1/4 teaspoons salt. Bring to a simmer, reduce the heat, and simmer, partially covered, until the chicken is just done, about 4 minutes. Remove the chicken and cover lightly with aluminum foil to keep warm. Set aside the pan with the broth.

2. Meanwhile, in a large pot of boiling, salted water, cook the orzo for 6 minutes. Add the carrots and continue cooking until the orzo and carrots are just done, about 6 minutes longer. Drain and toss with the remaining 1 tablespoon oil and 1/8 teaspoon each salt and pepper.

3. In a medium glass or stainless-steel bowl, beat the eggs, lemon juice, and 1/8 teaspoon of pepper until frothy. Bring the chicken broth back to a simmer and add to the eggs in a thin stream, whisking. Pour the mixture back into the pan and whisk over the lowest possible heat until the sauce begins to thicken, about 3 minutes. Do not let the sauce come to a simmer, or it may curdle. Put the orzo and carrots on plates and top with the chicken and sauce.

ORECCHIETTE WITH CHICKEN, CARAMELIZED ONIONS, AND BLUE CHEESE

The sweetness of the onions contrasts perfectly with the saltiness of the cheese in this exciting dish. Orecchiette (little ears) is a thick and satisfying pasta that we adore, but, if you like, you can use shells or bow ties instead.

WINE RECOMMENDATION
The onions and cheese drive the wine choice for this dish. A lighter red wine from the Piedmont region of Italy, such as one based on the barbera or dolcetto grapes, has the weight and acidity to stand up to the sweet and salty flavors.

SERVES 4

1	tablespoon butter
3	tablespoons olive oil
2	onions, quartered and cut into thin slices
1	teaspoon salt
1⅓	pounds boneless, skinless chicken breasts (about 4)
¼	teaspoon fresh-ground black pepper
¾	teaspoon dried rosemary, crumbled, or 2 teaspoons chopped fresh rosemary
1	clove garlic, minced
½	pound orecchiette
2	ounces blue cheese, crumbled (about ½ cup)

1. In a large nonstick frying pan, melt the butter with 2 tablespoons of oil over moderately high heat. Add the onions and ½ teaspoon of the salt and cook, stirring frequently, until well browned, about 25 minutes. Remove.

2. Add the remaining 1 tablespoon oil to the pan and reduce the heat to moderate. Season the chicken with ¼ teaspoon of the salt and ⅛ teaspoon of the pepper and add to the pan along with the rosemary. Cook the chicken until brown, about 5 minutes. Turn and cook until almost done, about 3 minutes longer. Add the garlic. Cook, stirring, for 30 seconds. Cover the pan, remove from the heat, and let steam for 5 minutes. Cut the chicken into ¼-inch slices.

3. Meanwhile, in a large pot of boiling, salted water, cook the orecchiette until just done, about 15 minutes. Reserve about ¼ cup of the pasta water. Drain the pasta and toss with 2 tablespoons of the pasta water, the onions, the chicken with pan juices, the blue cheese, and the remaining ¼ teaspoon salt and ⅛ teaspoon pepper. If the pasta seems dry, add more of the reserved pasta water.

FUSILLI WITH SPICY CHICKEN SAUSAGE, TOMATO, AND RICOTTA CHEESE

Hearty and comforting, this pasta makes a great meal for a cold winter evening. If you like, replace the hot sausages with mild ones, or use turkey sausage instead.

WINE RECOMMENDATION

The acidity of the tomato and spiciness of the sausage are best suited to a red wine with soft tannin and good acidity. Try a sangiovese from Tuscany such as Chianti Classico or Rosso di Montalcino or look for a version from California.

SERVES 4

1 tablespoon olive oil

1 pound hot chicken sausages

1 onion, chopped

2 cloves garlic, chopped

¼ cup dry white wine

1½ cups canned crushed tomatoes in thick puree

¼ cup water

¼ teaspoon dried rosemary, crumbled
   Pinch dried red-pepper flakes

½ teaspoon salt

3 tablespoons chopped flat-leaf parsley

½ pound fusilli

¾ cup ricotta cheese

1. In a large, deep frying pan, heat the oil over moderate heat. Add the sausage and cook, turning, until browned and cooked through, about 10 minutes. Remove the sausage and, when it is cool enough to handle, cut it into ¼-inch slices. Pour off all but 1 tablespoon fat from the pan.

2. Reduce the heat to moderately low. Add the onion to the pan and cook, stirring occasionally, until translucent, about 5 minutes. Add the garlic and cook 30 seconds longer.

3. Add the wine and bring to a simmer. Add the sausage, tomatoes, water, rosemary, red-pepper flakes, and ¼ teaspoon of the salt and bring to a simmer. Cook, stirring occasionally, for 10 minutes. Stir in the parsley.

4. Meanwhile, in a large pot of boiling, salted water, cook the fusilli until just done, about 13 minutes. Drain and toss with the sauce, the ricotta, and the remaining ¼ teaspoon salt.

CHICKEN PAD THAI

Our version of *pad thai*, the satisfying rice-noodle dish from Thailand, is made with chicken, tofu, bean sprouts, and, in place of hard-to-find rice noodles, linguine. The fish sauce is available at Asian markets and keeps forever. If you like, you can use a mixture of soy sauce and oyster sauce instead. Lime wedges make a nice final touch.

WINE RECOMMENDATION
Anything more than a straightforward white with some residual sugar would be pointless with the forceful flavors of the *pad thai*. A riesling from California or Australia will be fine.

SERVES 4

- 1 pound boneless, skinless chicken breasts (about 3), cut into 1-inch cubes
- 5 tablespoons plus 1 teaspoon Asian fish sauce
- ½ pound firm tofu, cut into ¼-inch cubes
- 1 cup water
- 2 tablespoons lime juice
- 1½ teaspoons rice-wine vinegar
- 3½ tablespoons sugar
- ¾ teaspoon salt
- ¼ teaspoon cayenne
- ¾ pound linguine
- 3 tablespoons cooking oil
- 4 cloves garlic, chopped
- ⅔ cup salted peanuts, chopped fine
- 2 cups bean sprouts
- ½ cup lightly packed cilantro leaves

1. In a small bowl, combine the chicken and ½ teaspoon of the fish sauce. In another bowl, combine the tofu with another ½ teaspoon of the fish sauce. In a medium glass or stainless-steel bowl, combine the remaining 5 tablespoons fish sauce with the water, 1½ tablespoons of the lime juice, the vinegar, sugar, salt, and cayenne.

2. In a pot of boiling, salted water, cook the linguine until done, about 12 minutes. Drain.

3. Meanwhile, in a wok or large frying pan, heat 1 tablespoon of the oil over moderately high heat. Add the chicken and cook, stirring, until just done, 3 to 4 minutes. Remove. Put another tablespoon of oil in the pan. Add the tofu and cook, stirring, for 2 minutes. Remove. Put the remaining 1 tablespoon oil in the pan, add the garlic and cook, stirring, for 30 seconds.

4. Add the pasta and the fish-sauce mixture. Cook, stirring, until nearly all the liquid is absorbed, about 3 minutes. Stir in the chicken, tofu, and ⅓ cup peanuts. Remove from the heat. Stir in the remaining ½ tablespoon lime juice, the bean sprouts, and half the cilantro. Top with the remaining peanuts and cilantro.

FETTUCCINE WITH TURKEY AND BRANDIED MUSHROOMS

A hint of brandy flavors the sautéed mushrooms. You might use port or sherry. For a special treat, try an assortment of wild mushrooms.

WINE RECOMMENDATION
A rich, oaky chardonnay will be ideal with the brandy and cream here. Good possibilities are those produced in Washington State, California, and Australia.

SERVES 4

1 tablespoon cooking oil

1 pound turkey cutlets (about 3)

1¼ teaspoons salt

½ teaspoon fresh-ground black pepper

2 tablespoons butter

2 scallions, white bulbs and green tops chopped separately

1 pound mushrooms, cut into thin slices

⅓ cup brandy

1 cup canned low-sodium chicken broth or homemade stock

½ pound fettuccine

¼ cup heavy cream

2 tablespoons chopped fresh parsley

1. In a large nonstick frying pan, heat the oil over moderately high heat. Season the turkey cutlets with ¼ teaspoon each of the salt and pepper. Cook the cutlets until they are almost done, about 1 minute per side. Remove the cutlets from the pan, let cool, and then cut them into thin strips.

2. Melt the butter in the same pan over moderate heat. Add the white part of the scallions, the mushrooms, ½ teaspoon of the salt, and the remaining ¼ teaspoon pepper. Cook, stirring occasionally, until the mushrooms let off their liquid and it evaporates, about 5 minutes. Add the brandy and cook until almost no liquid remains in the pan, about 2 minutes more. Add ½ cup of broth and simmer until almost completely evaporated, about 4 minutes.

3. In a large pot of boiling, salted water, cook the fettuccine until almost done, about 7 minutes. Drain the pasta and then add it to the mushrooms. Add the remaining ½ cup broth, the cream, the scallion tops, the remaining ½ teaspoon salt, and the turkey strips. Simmer until the turkey is just done, about 1 minute longer. Top with the parsley.

MENU SUGGESTION

A simple side dish of boiled or sautéed green beans is all that's needed.

CHICKEN AND ZUCCHINI COUSCOUS

A version of the North African classic, this recipe combines chicken, chickpeas, and zucchini in a cumin-spiced tomato broth. Traditionally chicken is braised in a special pot with a top compartment for steaming the couscous, but you can cook couscous, available at most supermarkets, in a saucepan in a matter of minutes.

WINE RECOMMENDATION
The aromatic spices in this dish are best with an assertive, flavorful wine; color is almost secondary. For a red, try a wine from the indigenous South African grape, pinotage. For white, try a Tokay Pinot Gris from Alsace in France.

SERVES 4

1 tablespoon olive oil

1 chicken (3 to 3½ pounds), cut into 8 pieces

1½ teaspoons salt

1 onion, chopped

4 cloves garlic, chopped

1 tablespoon chopped fresh ginger

½ teaspoon paprika

¾ teaspoon ground cumin

½ teaspoon dried oregano

¼ teaspoon cayenne

¼ teaspoon ground turmeric

1½ cups canned low-sodium chicken broth or homemade stock

1 cup canned crushed tomatoes in thick puree

1 cup canned chickpeas, drained and rinsed

1 zucchini, cut into ¼-inch slices

3 tablespoons chopped fresh parsley

1 tablespoon lemon juice

4 cups cooked couscous

1. In a large pot, heat the oil over moderately high heat. Season the chicken pieces with ¼ teaspoon of the salt and add them to the pot. Cook, turning, until browned, about 8 minutes in all. Remove. Pour off all but 1 tablespoon fat from the pot.

2. Reduce the heat to moderately low. Add the onion to the pot and cook, stirring occasionally, until translucent, about 5 minutes. Add the garlic, ginger, paprika, cumin, oregano, cayenne, and turmeric and cook, stirring, for 30 seconds.

3. Add the broth, tomatoes, and the remaining 1¼ teaspoons of salt, scraping the bottom of the pot to dislodge any browned bits. Add the chicken thighs and drumsticks. Bring to a simmer and cook, covered, for 10 minutes. Add the chicken breasts with any accumulated juices, the chickpeas, and the zucchini and bring back to a simmer. Cook, covered, until the chicken and zucchini are just done, about 12 minutes longer. Add the parsley and lemon juice and serve over the couscous.

MUSHROOM AND CHICKEN RISOTTO

If you're using canned chicken broth to make risotto, be sure it's *low-sodium*. The broth reduces at the same time that it's cooking into the rice, and regular canned broth would become much too salty.

WINE RECOMMENDATION
The mushrooms and Parmesan in this dish will go beautifully with one of the lighter red Burgundies, which have fruitiness, earthiness, and firm acidity.

SERVES 4

2 tablespoons butter

½ pound mushrooms, cut into thin slices

⅔ pound boneless, skinless chicken breasts (about 2), cut into ½-inch pieces

1 teaspoon salt

¼ teaspoon fresh-ground black pepper

5½ cups canned low-sodium chicken broth or homemade stock, more if needed

1 tablespoon cooking oil

½ cup chopped onion

1½ cups arborio rice

½ cup dry white wine

½ cup grated Parmesan cheese, plus more for serving

2 tablespoons chopped fresh parsley

1. In a large pot, heat the butter over moderate heat. Add the mushrooms. Cook, stirring frequently, until the mushrooms are browned, about 5 minutes. Add the chicken, ¼ teaspoon of the salt, and the pepper. Cook until the chicken is just done, 3 to 4 minutes. Remove the mixture from the pan. In a medium saucepan, bring the broth to a simmer.

2. In the large pot, heat the oil over moderately low heat. Add the onion and cook, stirring occasionally, until translucent, about 5 minutes. Add the rice and stir until it begins to turn opaque, about 2 minutes.

3. Add the wine and the remaining ¾ teaspoon salt to the rice. Cook, stirring frequently, until all of the wine has been absorbed. Add about ½ cup of the simmering broth and cook, stirring frequently, until it has been absorbed. The rice and broth should bubble gently; adjust the heat as needed. Continue cooking the rice, adding broth ½ cup at a time and allowing the rice to absorb it before adding the next ½ cup. Cook the rice in this way until tender, 25 to 30 minutes in all. The broth that hasn't been absorbed should be thickened by the starch from the rice. You may not need to use all the liquid, or you may need more broth or some water.

4. Stir in the chicken and mushrooms, the Parmesan, and the parsley and heat through. Serve the risotto with additional Parmesan.

RISOTTO WITH SMOKED TURKEY, LEEKS, AND MASCARPONE

The mascarpone gives this risotto its delectable creaminess. If you like, you can make a close substitute with two ounces of cream cheese, at room temperature, and seven ounces of heavy cream. Whir them in a blender just until smooth; don't blend the mixture too long or it may curdle. Also, you can use a large onion in place of the leeks.

WINE RECOMMENDATION

Go for an Italian white wine with good body and acidity to offset the creaminess here. Look for an Arneis from the Piedmont region or pinot grigios from the regions of Alto Adige or Collio.

SERVES 4

- 5 cups canned low-sodium chicken broth or homemade stock, more if needed
- 1 cup water, more if needed
- 3 tablespoons olive oil
- 1½ pounds leeks (about 3), white and light-green parts only, cut crosswise into thin slices and washed well
- 2 cups arborio rice
- ½ cup dry white wine
- 2 teaspoons salt
- 1 6-ounce piece smoked turkey, cut into ¼-inch dice
- 1 cup mascarpone cheese
- ¼ teaspoon fresh-ground black pepper

1. In a medium saucepan, bring the broth and water to a simmer.

2. In a large pot, heat the oil over moderately low heat. Add the leeks and cook, stirring occasionally, until translucent, about 10 minutes. Add the rice and stir until it begins to turn opaque, about 2 minutes.

3. Add the wine and salt to the rice and cook, stirring frequently, until all of the wine has been absorbed.

4. Add about ½ cup of the simmering broth to the rice and cook, stirring frequently, until the broth has been completely absorbed. The rice and broth should bubble gently; adjust the heat as needed. Continue cooking the rice, adding the broth ½ cup at a time and allowing the rice to absorb the stock before adding the next ½ cup. Cook the rice in this way until tender, 25 to 30 minutes in all. The broth that hasn't been absorbed should be thickened by the starch from the rice. You may not need to use all of the liquid, or you may need to add more broth or water. Add the turkey, cheese, and pepper.

Arroz con Pollo

Here's a perfect all-in-one meal—the chicken, rice, and vegetables simmer together, enhancing each other and giving the cook a break.

WINE RECOMMENDATION
This traditional Spanish favorite will work well with any smooth, full-flavored red, such as a merlot or zinfandel from California or a Rioja from Spain.

SERVES 4

- 1 tablespoon olive oil
- 4 chicken thighs
- 4 chicken drumsticks
- 2 teaspoons salt
- ½ teaspoon fresh-ground black pepper
- 2 ounces smoked ham, cut into ¼-inch dice
- 1 small onion, chopped
- 2 cloves garlic, minced
- 1 red bell pepper, chopped
- 1 green bell pepper, chopped
- 1¾ cups canned tomatoes, drained and chopped
- 1 tablespoon tomato paste
- 2 cups canned low-sodium chicken broth or homemade stock
- 1 cup rice, preferably long-grain
- 2 tablespoons chopped fresh parsley

1. In a large, deep frying pan, heat the oil over moderately high heat. Season the chicken with ¼ teaspoon each of the salt and pepper. Cook the chicken, turning, until well browned, about 8 minutes in all. Remove. Pour off all but 2 tablespoons of the fat from the pan.

2. Reduce the heat to moderately low. Add the ham, onion, and garlic to the pan and cook, stirring occasionally, until the onion starts to soften, about 2 minutes. Add the bell peppers and cook, stirring occasionally, until they start to soften, about 3 minutes longer.

3. Add the tomatoes, tomato paste, broth, and the remaining 1¾ teaspoons salt and ¼ teaspoon of the pepper and bring to a simmer. Stir in the rice and add the chicken in an even layer. Simmer, partially covered, over moderately low heat until the chicken and rice are just done, 20 to 25 minutes. Sprinkle with parsley.

CHICKEN WITH RICE AND BEANS

Three favorite Latin-American ingredients combine here to make one hearty and delicious dish that's welcome any time of year. We recommend Goya canned black beans, which hold up during cooking better than other brands do.

WINE RECOMMENDATION
A fruity red wine such as a merlot is best with this classic dish. If you can, try to find a bottle from a producer in Argentina or Chile, or open your favorite California merlot.

SERVES 4

    1   tablespoon cooking oil
    4   chicken thighs
    4   chicken drumsticks
1¾   teaspoons salt
    ¼   teaspoon fresh-ground black pepper
    1   onion, chopped fine
    2   cloves garlic, minced
    1   cup canned crushed tomatoes
    ½   cup bottled pimientos, drained
1⅔   cups drained and rinsed black beans
        (from one 15-ounce can)
    1   cup rice, preferably medium-grain
1¾   cups water
    2   tablespoons chopped fresh parsley
    ⅛   teaspoon cayenne
    4   lime wedges (optional)

1. In a large, deep frying pan, heat the oil over moderately high heat. Season the chicken with ¼ teaspoon of the salt and the pepper and add to the pan. Cook, turning, until well browned, about 8 minutes in all. Remove. Pour off all but 1 tablespoon of the fat from the pan.

2. Add the onion to the pan and reduce the heat to moderately low. Cook, stirring occasionally, until translucent, about 5 minutes. Add the garlic and cook, stirring, for 30 seconds longer. Add the tomatoes and pimientos, scraping the bottom of the pan to dislodge any brown bits. Stir in the beans, rice, water, parsley, the remaining 1½ teaspoons of salt, and the cayenne, and arrange the chicken on top in an even layer.

3. Bring to a boil and simmer until all the water is absorbed, about 12 minutes. Turn the drumsticks and reduce the heat to very low. Cover and cook until the chicken and rice are just done, about 15 minutes longer. Serve with the lime wedges if using.

TURKEY SAUSAGE WITH CHEDDAR-CHEESE GRITS AND TOMATO SAUCE

Creamy, cheesy grits capture the juices from the fresh tomatoes making a perfect foil for the sausage links. Chicken sausage also works well in this homey combination.

WINE RECOMMENDATION
A simple, refreshing white wine is a nice contrast to the rich cheddar flavor of the grits. Try a pinot bianco from the Veneto region of Italy or a pinot blanc from Alsace in France.

SERVES 4

3½ cups water

1 teaspoon salt

¾ cup old-fashioned grits

¼ pound cheddar cheese, grated

1 tablespoon cooking oil

1 pound turkey sausages

1½ pounds tomatoes, chopped (about 2 cups)

¼ teaspoon fresh-ground black pepper

2 tablespoons chopped fresh parsley

1. In a medium saucepan, bring the water and ¾ teaspoon salt to a boil. Add the grits in a slow stream, whisking. Reduce the heat, cover, and simmer, stirring frequently with a wooden spoon, until the grits are very thick, about 20 minutes. Remove the saucepan from the heat and stir in the cheese.

2. Meanwhile, in a medium, nonstick frying pan, heat the oil over moderately low heat. Add the sausages and cook until they are just done, about 15 minutes. Remove the sausages from the pan. Add the tomatoes, the remaining ¼ teaspoon salt and the pepper to the pan. Cook until the tomatoes are just heated through, 1 to 2 minutes. Stir in the parsley.

3. Serve the grits topped with the sausages and the tomato sauce.

MENU SUGGESTIONS

Vegetables such as okra, lima beans, or cooked greens would be perfectly in keeping with the Southern theme.

CHAPTER FIVE

Salads
&
Sandwiches

GRILLED CHICKEN AND VEGETABLE SALAD WITH LEMON AND PEPPER VINAIGRETTE

Cool mixed greens topped with hot grilled chicken, carrots, and shiitake mushrooms make a great light meal. You can also let the grilled vegetables and chicken cool and serve them at room temperature.

WINE RECOMMENDATION
Look for a wine that has plenty of acidity to stand up to the vinaigrette. In the warmer months, a white such as a California sauvignon blanc or an Italian pinot grigio will taste best. If you prefer a red wine, try a gamay or pinot noir from California.

SERVES 4

⅓ cup plus 3 tablespoons olive oil

1 teaspoon dried thyme

1 pound boneless, skinless chicken breasts (about 3)

1 teaspoon salt

¾ teaspoon fresh-ground black pepper

¼ pound shiitake mushrooms, stems removed

4 carrots, cut diagonally into ¼-inch slices

½ teaspoon Dijon mustard

4 teaspoons lemon juice

2 heads leaf lettuce, torn into bite-size pieces (about 3 quarts)

2 scallions including green tops, chopped

1. Light the grill. In a small bowl, combine the 3 tablespoons oil and the thyme. Coat the chicken with about 1 tablespoon of the thyme oil and sprinkle with ¼ teaspoon of the salt and ⅛ teaspoon of the pepper. Grill the chicken over moderately high heat until just done, about 4 minutes per side. Remove and let rest for 5 minutes, and cut diagonally into ¼-inch pieces.

2. In a medium bowl, toss the mushrooms and carrots with the remaining thyme oil, ¼ teaspoon of the salt, and ⅛ teaspoon of the pepper. Grill the vegetables over moderately high heat, turning, until just done, about 4 minutes per side for the carrots and 6 minutes per side for the mushrooms.

3. In a small glass or stainless-steel bowl, whisk together the mustard, lemon juice, and the remaining ½ teaspoon salt and ½ teaspoon pepper. Whisk in the remaining ⅓ cup oil.

4. In a large bowl, combine the lettuce, half of the scallions, and all but 2 tablespoons of the vinaigrette. Mound onto plates. Top with the vegetables and chicken. Drizzle the remaining vinaigrette over the chicken and top with the remaining scallions.

VIETNAMESE CHICKEN SALAD

Bold flavors star in this Vietnamese salad—acidic lime juice, hot pepper, salty soy sauce, and cooling herbs. The combination of mint and cilantro is typical and refreshing, but you can use only one herb, or leave them both out completely if you prefer.

WINE RECOMMENDATION

A lively, acidic white wine that has no oak flavor will be best with the spices and greens in this dish. Try a sauvignon blanc from South Africa or Australia or a pinot grigio from Italy.

SERVES 4

1⅓ pounds boneless, skinless chicken breasts (about 4)

1 cup canned low-sodium chicken broth or homemade stock

4 scallions including green tops, chopped

½ teaspoon salt

1¼ pounds green cabbage (about ½ head), shredded (about 4 cups)

3 carrots, grated

6 tablespoons chopped fresh mint and/or cilantro (optional)

¼ cup lime juice (from about 2 limes)

¼ cup soy sauce or Asian fish sauce (nam pla or nuoc mam)*

4 teaspoons sugar

¼ teaspoon dried red-pepper flakes

¼ cup chopped peanuts

*Available at Asian markets and some supermarkets

1. Cut each chicken breast into five diagonal strips. In a medium saucepan, combine the broth, ¼ of the scallions, and ¼ teaspoon of the salt. Bring to a simmer, add the chicken, stir, and cover the pan. Cook over low heat for 5 minutes. Turn the heat off and let the chicken steam for 5 minutes. Remove the chicken from the pan and shred it.

2. In a large bowl, combine the shredded chicken, the remaining scallions, the cabbage, carrots, and 4 tablespoons of the herbs, if using. In a small glass or stainless-steel bowl, whisk together the lime juice, soy sauce, sugar, red-pepper flakes, and the remaining ¼ teaspoon salt. Toss the salad with the dressing. Sprinkle with the remaining 2 tablespoons chopped herbs and the peanuts.

MENU SUGGESTIONS

This crunchy, Asian-flavored salad will taste even more refreshing served with tropical fruit, such as pineapple, mango, papaya, or star fruit.

Spinach Salad with Smoked Chicken, Apple, Walnuts, and Bacon

Celebrate autumn's apple season with this delicious and substantial salad. We call for the thick-sliced, smoked chicken now available in the meat department of supermarkets. Of course, you can always use smoked turkey from the deli counter instead. If you like a more pronounced sweet-and-sour flavor, use another teaspoon of vinegar.

WINE RECOMMENDATION
This substantial fall salad, with its hearty flavors, will taste great with a Beaujolais or, for something off the beaten path, a fruity pinotage from South Africa. In either case, chill the bottle for fifteen minutes or so before serving.

SERVES 4

¾ cup walnuts, chopped

¼ pound sliced bacon

2 tablespoons red-wine vinegar

1 teaspoon Dijon mustard

¾ teaspoon salt

¼ teaspoon fresh-ground black pepper

⅓ cup cooking oil

⅔ pound smoked and sliced boneless chicken breast

1 pound spinach, stems removed, leaves washed (about 9 cups)

1 small red onion, chopped fine

1 tart apple, such as Granny Smith, peeled, cored, and cut into ½-inch pieces

1. Heat the oven to 350°. Toast the walnuts until golden brown, about 8 minutes. Let cool.

2. In a large frying pan, cook the bacon until it is crisp. Drain the bacon on paper towels and then crumble it.

3. In a small glass or stainless-steel bowl, whisk the vinegar with the mustard, salt, and pepper. Whisk in the oil.

4. In a large bowl, combine 2 tablespoons of the dressing with the chicken. Let sit for about 5 minutes so that the chicken absorbs the dressing. Add the walnuts, bacon, spinach, onion, apple, and the remaining dressing and toss.

Menu Suggestions

Hot garlic bread, served either plain or with a little Parmesan cheese, goes well with all the flavors here.

SESAME CHICKEN SALAD

Sesame sauce bathes layers of chicken, cucumber, and noodles in this satisfying main-course salad. Assemble the salad just before serving, or the cucumbers will release liquid, turn limp, and make the sauce watery.

WINE RECOMMENDATION
The bold flavors of the salad will be complemented by the acidity and slight sweetness of a German kabinett riesling from the Mosel-Saar-Ruwer.

SERVES 4

¼ pound vermicelli

1 cup plus 3 tablespoons canned low-sodium chicken broth or homemade stock

3 scallions including green tops, cut into ¼-inch slices

¼ teaspoon salt

1⅓ pounds boneless, skinless chicken breasts (about 4)

1 tablespoon chopped fresh ginger

4 cloves garlic, chopped

2 tablespoons tahini (sesame-seed paste)

1 tablespoon Asian sesame oil

2 teaspoons sugar

2½ tablespoons cooking oil

⅛ teaspoon dried red-pepper flakes

3 tablespoons soy sauce

½ teaspoon fresh-ground black pepper

2 cucumbers, halved lengthwise, peeled, and seeded

1. In a pot of boiling, salted water, cook the vermicelli until just done, about 9 minutes. Drain Rinse with cold water; drain thoroughly.

2. In a medium saucepan, combine the 1 cup broth, one third of the scallions, and the salt. Bring to a simmer, add the chicken, stir, and cover the pan. Simmer for 5 minutes. Turn the heat off and let the chicken steam for 5 minutes. Remove the chicken from the saucepan and shred it.

3. In a blender, puree the remaining 3 tablespoons broth, the ginger, garlic, tahini, sesame oil, sugar, cooking oil, red-pepper flakes, soy sauce, and pepper. Put the cucumber halves cut-side down and slice them lengthwise into thin strips.

4. To serve, put the vermicelli on plates or in bowls. Scatter each serving with a layer of cucumber strips and then top with the shredded chicken. Pour the sesame sauce over the chicken and sprinkle with the remaining scallions.

MOROCCAN CHICKEN AND POTATO SALAD WITH OLIVES

A savory lemon dressing with cumin, paprika, ginger, and oregano gives this salad an exotic flavor. Serve the salad warm or at room temperature.

WINE RECOMMENDATION
This dish would be wonderful with a well-chilled bottle of rosé, which will refresh the palate without interfering with the salad's flavors. Look for a bottle from Bandol, Cassis, or elsewhere in the South of France.

SERVES 4

1½   pounds boiling potatoes (about 5)

1½   tablespoons lemon juice

1   teaspoon ground cumin

1   teaspoon paprika

1   teaspoon salt

    Fresh-ground black pepper

¼   teaspoon ground ginger

¼   teaspoon dried oregano

7   tablespoons olive oil

1   pound boneless, skinless chicken breasts (about 3)

½   red onion, chopped fine

⅓   cup black olives, such as Kalamata, halved and pitted

½   cup chopped flat-leaf parsley

1. Put the potatoes in a medium saucepan with salted water to cover and bring to a boil. Reduce the heat and cook at a gentle boil until tender about 25 minutes. Drain the potatoes. When they are cool enough to handle, peel the potatoes and cut into ¼-inch slices.

2. Meanwhile, in a small glass or stainless-steel bowl, whisk together the lemon juice, cumin, paprika, ¾ teaspoon of the salt, ¼ teaspoon pepper, the ginger, and the oregano. Whisk in 6 tablespoons of the oil.

3. Heat a grill pan or a heavy frying pan over moderate heat. For the grill pan, coat the chicken with the remaining 1 tablespoon oil; sprinkle with the remaining ¼ teaspoon salt and ⅛ teaspoon pepper. Cook the chicken for 5 minutes. Turn and cook until browned and just done, about 4 minutes longer. Remove, and when cool enough to handle, cut the chicken into ¼-inch slices. For the frying pan, heat the oil in the pan and then season, cook, and slice the chicken in the same way.

4. In a large bowl, combine the warm potatoes with half of the dressing. Add the chicken, onion, olives, parsley, and the remaining dressing and toss.

159

SOUTHWESTERN TORTILLA SALAD

This Tex-Mex favorite comes together in minutes. You'll be surprised by how quick and easy it is to make your own refried beans—and how much better they taste than the ready-made variety.

WINE RECOMMENDATION
The forceful flavor of cheddar cheese and the saltiness of the olives will go very nicely with a crisp and lively sauvignon blanc from California.

SERVES 4

8 taco shells

5½ tablespoons cooking oil

2 cups drained and rinsed kidney beans (from one 19-ounce can)

⅓ cup tomato salsa

¾ teaspoon salt

1½ tablespoons wine vinegar

¾ teaspoon Dijon mustard

¼ teaspoon fresh-ground black pepper

¼ teaspoon chili powder

¼ cup chopped cilantro (optional)

1 head romaine lettuce, shredded

2 large tomatoes, chopped

1 avocado, cut into thin slices

¼ pound cheddar cheese, grated (about 1 cup)

1 roasted chicken, bones and skin removed, meat shredded (about 1 pound meat)

⅓ cup black olives, such as Kalamata, halved and pitted

1. Heat the oven to 350°. Put the taco shells on a baking sheet and bake them until crisp, about 8 minutes. Break each one in half.

2. In a medium saucepan, heat 1 tablespoon of the oil over moderate heat. Add the beans, salsa, and ¼ teaspoon of the salt. Cook, mashing with a potato masher, for about 5 minutes.

3. In a small glass or stainless-steel bowl, whisk together the vinegar, mustard, pepper, chili powder, and the remaining ½ teaspoon salt. Add the remaining 4½ tablespoons oil, whisking. Add the cilantro.

4. To serve, spread one side of the taco-shell halves with the refried beans and put four on each plate. Top with layers of the lettuce, tomatoes, avocado, cheese, chicken, and olives. Pour the dressing over the salads.

CHICKEN BURRITOS WITH BLACK-BEAN SALSA AND PEPPER JACK

Pepper Jack cheese looks innocent enough but adds a nice kick to these burritos. If you prefer a milder taste, use regular Jack instead.

WINE RECOMMENDATION

With the heat from the cheese, stay away from any serious, high-alcohol, low-acid wines. Try a white from a cooler growing area such as a riesling from the Finger Lakes region of New York or any white from the Alto Adige region of Italy. A cold beer is a great alternative.

SERVES 4

1²/₃   cups drained and rinsed black beans (from one 15-ounce can)

2   scallions including green tops, chopped

1   tablespoon lemon or lime juice

¼   teaspoon ground cumin

½   teaspoon salt

1¹/₃   pounds boneless, skinless chicken breasts (about 4)

¼   teaspoon chili powder

¼   teaspoon fresh-ground black pepper

½   pound pepper Jack cheese, grated

4   large (9-inch) flour tortillas

1. Light the grill or heat the broiler. In a small glass or stainless-steel bowl, combine the beans, scallions, lemon juice, cumin, and ¼ teaspoon of the salt.

2. Rub the chicken breasts with the chili powder, pepper, and the remaining ¼ teaspoon salt. Cook the chicken over moderate heat for 5 minutes. Turn and cook until brown and just done, 4 to 5 minutes longer. Remove, let the chicken rest for a few minutes, and then slice.

3. Heat the oven to 350°. Put one quarter of the cheese in a line near one edge of each tortilla. Top the cheese with one quarter of the black-bean salsa and then with one quarter of the chicken slices. Roll up the burritos and wrap each one in foil. Bake them until the cheese melts, about 15 minutes.

DO-AHEAD TIP

You can assemble the burritos ahead of time and bake them just before serving. If they've been in the refrigerator, add about five minutes to the baking time.

MENU SUGGESTIONS

Embellish your burritos with sour cream or salsa, if you like. Sliced tomatoes or rice would make good side dishes.

CHICKEN AND FETA TOSTADAS

A Mexican classic with a Greek twist, these tostadas appeal to children of all ages. If you can't buy roasted chicken ready-made, use leftover chicken or cook some according to whichever of the methods on pages 180 to 181 seems easiest to you. Serve one burrito-size tortilla or two of the smaller ones per person.

WINE RECOMMENDATION
The saltiness of the feta cheese and olives and the tartness of the tomatoes will pair well with the crisp acidity in a sauvignon blanc from either the Loire Valley or a northern region of Italy such as Collio or Veneto.

SERVES 4

¾ pound plum tomatoes, chopped

½ cup black olives, such as Kalamata, pitted and chopped

¼ cup chopped fresh parsley

1 roasted chicken, bones and skin removed, meat shredded (about 1 pound boneless meat)

½ teaspoon salt

½ teaspoon fresh-ground black pepper

2 tablespoons red-wine vinegar

3 tablespoons cooking oil, plus more for brushing tortillas

8 small or 4 large flour tortillas

½ pound feta cheese, crumbled (about 2 cups)

1. Heat the oven to 450°. In a large glass or stainless-steel bowl, combine the tomatoes, olives, parsley, chicken, salt, pepper, vinegar, and the 3 tablespoons oil.

2. Brush the tortillas on both sides with oil and then put on baking sheets, overlapping if necessary. Bake the tortillas until starting to brown, 2 to 3 minutes. Turn the tortillas and brown the other side, 2 to 3 minutes longer.

3. Remove the baking sheets from the oven and top each tortilla with an equal amount of the feta cheese. Return the baking sheets to the oven; cook until the cheese is just melting, 1 to 2 minutes longer. Top the tortillas with the chicken mixture.

MENU SUGGESTIONS

A fruit salad would be an easy and complementary accompaniment.

CHICKEN SOUVLAKI

Grilled chicken on pita with tomatoes, onions, and *tzatziki*, a yogurt and cucumber sauce, makes a cool yet satisfying warm-weather supper. Souvlaki is often rolled to eat in your hand as a snack, but this more substantial version is served on a plate with a knife and fork. If you like, accompany the souvlaki with lemon wedges. When using wooden skewers, soak them first in water for at least ten minutes, or they'll smoke during cooking.

WINE RECOMMENDATION
This traditional Greek preparation goes with a number of choices to suit the occasion and your taste. Look for a very fruity red such as a Beaujolais, a sparkling wine from California, or a sauvignon blanc from northern Italy.

SERVES 4

2 cups plain yogurt

1 cucumber, halved lengthwise, peeled, seeded, and grated

1¼ teaspoons salt

1 clove garlic, minced

Fresh-ground black pepper

¼ teaspoon dried dill

2 tablespoons olive oil

1½ teaspoons lemon juice

1 tablespoon dried oregano

1⅓ pounds boneless, skinless chicken breasts (about 4), cut into 1-inch cubes

4 pocketless pitas

6 tablespoons butter, at room temperature

1 small onion, cut into thin wedges

2 tomatoes, cut into thin wedges

⅓ cup black olives, such as Kalamata, halved and pitted

1. Put the yogurt in a strainer lined with cheesecloth, a coffee filter, or a paper towel and set it over a bowl. Let drain in the refrigerator for 15 minutes. In a medium glass or stainless-steel bowl, combine the cucumber with 1 teaspoon of the salt; let sit for about 15 minutes. Squeeze the cucumber to remove the liquid. Put the cucumber back in the bowl and stir in the drained yogurt, the garlic, ⅛ teaspoon of pepper, and the dill.

2. Light the grill or heat the broiler. In a small glass or stainless-steel bowl, combine the oil, lemon juice, oregano, the remaining ¼ teaspoon of salt, and ¼ teaspoon of pepper. Toss the chicken cubes in the oil mixture and thread them onto skewers. Grill the chicken over high heat or broil, turning once, until done, about 5 minutes in all. Transfer the chicken to a plate.

3. Spread both sides of the pitas with the butter and grill or broil, turning once, until golden, about 4 minutes in all. Cut into quarters.

4. To serve, put the pitas on plates and top with the onion, tomatoes, and chicken skewers with any accumulated juices. Serve with the *tzatziki* and olives.

SPICY PITA POCKETS WITH CHICKEN, LENTILS, AND TAHINI SAUCE

Here's something great to do with roasted chicken from the deli—a Middle Eastern sandwich chock-full of spicy lentils, bulgur, lettuce, tomato, and tahini sauce. Two pockets per person is enough to make a meal. If you like, serve extra Tabasco sauce at the table. You can find tahini (sesame-seed paste) in most supermarkets.

WINE RECOMMENDATION

You need a straightforward wine that won't compete but will be gulpable enough to prepare the palate for the next hot bite. Try a chenin blanc or a white zinfandel from California.

SERVES 4

1 cup dried lentils

½ onion, cut in half

2¾ cups plus 6 tablespoons water

1 tablespoon olive oil

2½ teaspoons salt

1 bay leaf

½ cup coarse bulgur

1½ teaspoons Tabasco sauce

½ cup tahini

2 cloves garlic, minced

5 teaspoons lemon juice

1 cup plain yogurt

8 pitas

1 roasted chicken, bones and skin removed, meat shredded (about 1 pound meat)

2 large tomatoes, chopped

1 head romaine lettuce, shredded

1. Heat the oven to 350°. In a medium saucepan, combine the lentils, onion, the 2¾ cups water, the oil, 1 teaspoon of the salt, and the bay leaf. Bring to a boil; simmer, partially covered, for 15 minutes. Stir in the bulgur and continue cooking, partially covered, stirring occasionally, until the lentils and bulgur are just done, about 12 more minutes. Remove from the heat, stir in the Tabasco sauce, and let sit, partially covered, for 5 minutes. Remove the onion and the bay leaf.

2. Meanwhile, in a medium glass or stainless-steel bowl, whisk together the tahini, the remaining 6 tablespoons water, the garlic, the lemon juice, the remaining 1½ teaspoons salt, and the yogurt.

3. Wrap the pitas in aluminum foil and warm them in the oven, about 10 minutes.

4. Cut the top third off of each pita. Spoon ¼ cup of the lentil mixture into each pita. Divide half the chicken and tomatoes among the pitas and drizzle each with 1 tablespoon of the sauce. Top with half the lettuce. Repeat. Serve with the remaining sauce.

CHICKEN PAN BAGNAT

Literally *bathed bread* in the ancient dialect of Provence, *pan bagnat* delivers meat, bread, and salad all in one handful. You both brush the bread with oil and let the finished rolls sit for a few minutes to allow the dressing to permeate the bread and bathe it with flavor.

WINE RECOMMENDATION
The south-of-France flavor of this sandwich is perfect with the delicate, herbal notes found in many rosés from Provence. Bottles from the Coteaux du Varois, Cassis, or Bandol would all be good possibilities.

SERVES 4

1   tablespoon lemon juice

2   teaspoons chopped fresh thyme, or ¾ teaspoon dried thyme

¾   teaspoon salt

¾   teaspoon fresh-ground black pepper

⅓   cup plus 2 tablespoons olive oil

4   large, crusty rolls, cut in half

1   large clove garlic, cut in half

8   large, crisp lettuce leaves, such as Boston

2   large tomatoes, sliced thin

1   roasted chicken, bones and skin removed, meat shredded (about 1 pound meat)

2   hard-cooked eggs, sliced

1   red onion, sliced thin

1   green bell pepper, sliced thin

⅓   cup black olives, such as Kalamata, halved and pitted

8   anchovy fillets (optional)

1. In a small glass or stainless-steel bowl, whisk together the lemon juice, thyme, ½ teaspoon each of the salt and pepper. Whisk in the ⅓ cup of oil.

2. Remove the soft centers of the rolls, leaving a ½-inch shell. Rub the garlic on the inside of each and brush with the 2 tablespoons oil.

3. Top the bottoms of the rolls with the lettuce. Layer with half the tomato slices and the chicken; sprinkle with ⅛ teaspoon each of salt and pepper. Top with half the slices of egg, onion, and bell pepper, and half the olives, and then drizzle with half the dressing. Repeat with the remaining tomato, chicken, ⅛ teaspoon each salt and pepper, egg, onion, bell pepper, olives, and dressing. Top with the anchovies, if using. Cover with the tops of the rolls. If you have time, wrap each roll tightly in aluminum foil; let sit for 10 minutes. Otherwise, press down on the rolls firmly so that the dressing moistens the bread.

MENU SUGGESTIONS

You really don't need anything with this, but roasted potato wedges would be nice.

TURKEY BURGERS

The focaccia adds to the Italian flavor of these juicy burgers. However, bread selections are endless—toasted country bread, onion rolls, or whatever you like.

WINE RECOMMENDATION

This meaty sandwich should be paired with a fresh, full-flavored red, perhaps one made from the versatile, food-friendly barbera grape. Several are imported from Italy's Piedmont region.

SERVES 4

1½ pounds ground turkey

¼ cup dry bread crumbs

¼ cup grated Parmesan cheese

¼ cup chopped fresh parsley

2 scallions including green tops, chopped
Salt

¼ teaspoon fresh-ground black pepper

2 tablespoons milk

1 egg, beaten to mix

2 tablespoons cooking oil

¼ pound provolone cheese, sliced

½ cup mayonnaise

3 tablespoons pesto, store-bought or homemade

1 10-inch round or 8-by-10-inch rectangle of focaccia

½ pound tomatoes, sliced

1. In a medium bowl, combine the ground turkey, bread crumbs, Parmesan cheese, parsley, scallions, ¾ teaspoon salt, the pepper, milk, and egg. Form the mixture into four patties, each about 1-inch thick.

2. In a large nonstick frying pan, heat the oil over moderate heat. Add the turkey burgers and cook for 5 minutes. Turn and then top each burger with the provolone cheese. Cook until just done, about 6 minutes longer.

3. Meanwhile, in a small bowl, combine the mayonnaise and the pesto. Cut the focaccia into quarters. Cut each piece in half horizontally. Spread the cut surfaces of each piece with the pesto mayonnaise.

4. Top the bottoms of the focaccia with the turkey burgers and then the tomato slices. Sprinkle the tomato with a pinch of salt. Cover with the top piece of focaccia.

MENU SUGGESTIONS

Burgers go best with other finger food—oven-roasted potato wedges and raw carrot or fennel sticks, for example.

SMOKED TURKEY AND SLAW ON COUNTRY TOAST

A simple slaw complements deli turkey in this tempting sandwich. Experiment with different breads, such as toasted sourdough, rye, or pita.

WINE RECOMMENDATION
Serve a simple, flavorful wine, such as a barrel-fermented sauvignon blanc from California or a pinot blanc from Alsace in France.

SERVES 4

- 2 tablespoons wine vinegar
- 1 pound red cabbage (about ⅓ head), shredded (about 1 quart)
- 2 carrots, grated
- ½ cup mayonnaise
- ¼ teaspoon ground cumin
- ¼ teaspoon paprika
- ¼ teaspoon salt
- ¼ teaspoon fresh-ground black pepper
- 8 thick slices from 1 large round loaf of country bread
- 1 pound smoked turkey, sliced thin
- 1 pound tomatoes, sliced

1. In a medium stainless-steel saucepan, heat the vinegar over moderate heat. Add the red cabbage and toss until it is starting to wilt, 1 to 2 minutes. Transfer the cabbage to a medium glass or stainless-steel bowl and toss with the carrots, mayonnaise, cumin, paprika, salt, and pepper.

2. Heat the broiler. Put the bread on a baking sheet and broil, turning once, until crisp on the outside but still slightly soft in the center, about 3 minutes in all. Sandwich the turkey, sliced tomato, and slaw between pieces of toast.

MENU SUGGESTIONS

Sandwiches need simple, no-fuss companions, such as oven fries, chips, or fruit salad.

VARIATIONS

Embellish the slaw as you like. Chopped scallions, grated jicama, or thin slices of green pepper all make good additions.

Multiply Your Options

Look to this section for practical help in deciding what ingredients to keep on hand, choosing the easiest way to cook your chicken, and planning how to serve it. Among the useful guides, you'll find ideas for making salads and simply sauced dishes and, for those times when you can't think what to do with the remainders of a roast chicken or turkey, a list of recipes in which you can include leftovers.

RECIPES PICTURED OPPOSITE: *(top)* pages 63, 47, 23; *(center)* pages 155, 41, 57; *(bottom)* pages 147, 131, 171

THE QUICK PANTRY

If you keep basic staples on hand, you can cut shopping to a minimum. Then you'll only have to make one short stop to pick up the fresh vegetables and poultry you need to complete the recipe.

CUPBOARD

- apple cider or juice
- apricots, dried
- beans, canned: black, chickpeas, kidney, white
- bread crumbs
- bulgar
- chicken broth, low-sodium
- coconut milk, unsweetened
- couscous
- figs, dried
- garlic
- grits, old-fashioned
- honey
- lentils
- maple syrup
- oil: cooking, olive

- onions
- pasta, dried: various shapes
- peanut butter
- pimiento
- potatoes
- raisins
- rice: arborio, long or medium grain
- soy sauce
- Tabasco sauce
- taco shells
- tomatoes: canned, paste, sun-dried
- vinegar: balsamic, red- or white-wine, rice-wine

SPICE SHELF

- allspice
- bay leaves
- cayenne
- chili powder
- cinnamon
- cloves
- coriander, ground and seeds
- cumin
- curry powder
- dill
- five-spice powder
- ginger
- marjoram
- mustard, dry
- nutmeg
- oregano
- paprika
- red-pepper flakes
- rosemary
- sage
- sesame seeds
- tarragon
- thyme
- turmeric

LIQUOR CABINET

- bourbon
- brandy
- port
- sherry
- vermouth, dry white
- wine: dry white, red

FREEZER

- bacon
- frozen vegetables: Brussels sprouts, okra, spinach
- nuts: peanuts, pecans, pine nuts, walnuts
- pasta

REFRIGERATOR

- anchovy paste
- apples
- butter
- capers
- cheese: Parmesan
- cream
- eggs
- fish sauce, Asian
- ginger, fresh
- jalapeño peppers
- ketchup
- lemons
- limes
- mayonnaise
- mustard: Dijon or grainy
- olives: black, green
- oranges
- parsley
- pesto
- salsa
- scallions
- sesame oil, Asian
- sour cream
- tahini
- yogurt, plain

LEFTOVERS

You can use leftover chicken or turkey in any of the recipes listed here. Substitute either one for the poultry called for in the ingredient list and add the meat when the dish is almost finished so that it just reheats rather than overcooks.

Basic Chicken-Cooking Methods

Some of our recipes call for store-bought roast chicken. If you'd rather cook your own, use any of the following methods. You'll find these recipes handy not only when you need cooked meat but when you want to serve plain chicken, embellish it with a pan sauce or compound butter, or make chicken salad (see pages 182 and 183).

ROASTED WHOLE CHICKEN

1   chicken (3 to 3½ pounds)
½   teaspoon salt
¼   teaspoon fresh-ground black pepper
1   tablespoon cooking oil

Heat the oven to 425°. Rub the bird inside and out with the salt and pepper. Twist the wings behind the back; tie the legs together. Put the chicken, breast-side up, in a roasting pan. Coat the chicken with the oil. Roast the chicken until done, about 55 minutes. Let the bird rest at least 10 minutes before cutting.

INDIVIDUAL SERVINGS

These recipes render about one pound of chicken meat. If you are serving individual pieces to four people, increase the number of thighs from six to eight, or replace the thighs with four whole legs. Add a few more minutes cooking time if you use legs.

BONE-IN BREASTS OR THIGHS

BAKED

4   bone-in chicken breasts or 6 thighs
1   tablespoon cooking oil
¼   teaspoon salt
⅛   teaspoon fresh-ground black pepper

Heat the oven to 400°. Coat the chicken with the oil; season with the salt and pepper. Put the chicken, skin-side up, in a roasting pan. Bake until just done, about 25 minutes for the breasts and 30 minutes for the thighs.

GRILLED

4   bone-in chicken breasts or 6 thighs
3   tablespoons cooking oil
¼   teaspoon salt
⅛   teaspoon fresh-ground black pepper

Light the grill. Coat the chicken with 1 tablespoon of the oil and season with the salt and pepper. Grill over moderately high heat, basting with the remaining 2 tablespoons oil, until just done, about 10 minutes per side for breasts and 12 per side for thighs.

POACHED

- 2 cups canned low-sodium chicken broth or homemade stock
- ½ teaspoon salt
- 4 bone-in chicken breasts or 6 thighs

In a large frying pan, combine the broth and salt and bring to a simmer. Add the chicken in a single layer and simmer, covered, for 10 minutes for breasts, 15 for thighs. Remove the pan from the heat. Let the chicken steam until just done, about 5 minutes, and remove from the broth. Strain the flavorful broth for later use.

BONELESS, SKINLESS BREASTS OR THIGHS

SAUTÉED

- 1 tablespoon cooking oil
- 4 boneless, skinless chicken breasts, or 6 boneless, skinless thighs
- ¼ teaspoon salt
- ⅛ teaspoon fresh-ground black pepper

In a large nonstick frying pan, heat the oil over moderate heat. Season the chicken with the salt and pepper, add to the pan, and cook until brown, about 5 minutes. Turn and cook until almost done, about 3 minutes longer for breasts and 5 for thighs. Cover the pan, remove from the heat, and let steam 5 minutes.

GRILLED

- 4 boneless, skinless chicken breasts, or 6 boneless, skinless thighs
- 3 tablespoons cooking oil
- ¼ teaspoon salt
- ⅛ teaspoon fresh-ground black pepper

Light the grill. Coat the chicken with 1 tablespoon of the oil and season with the salt and pepper. Grill the chicken over moderately high heat, basting with the remaining 2 tablespoons oil, until just done, about 5 minutes per side for breasts and 7 minutes per side for thighs.

POACHED

- 2 cups canned low-sodium chicken broth or homemade stock
- ½ teaspoon salt
- 4 boneless, skinless chicken breasts, or 6 boneless, skinless thighs

In a large frying pan, combine the broth and salt and bring to a simmer. Add the chicken in a single layer and simmer, covered, for 5 minutes for breasts, 10 for thighs. Remove the pan from the heat, let the chicken steam for 5 minutes longer, and remove from the broth. Strain the flavorful broth for later use.

Infinite Possibilities

PAN SAUCES

An easy way to make a quick meal is to sauté your favorite chicken parts and finish them off with a simple pan sauce. The technique is easy; just adapt it to what you like and have on hand.

1. **SAUTÉ** chicken in a little oil or a combination of oil and butter. Remove chicken from the pan.

2. **ADD** aromatic vegetables and cook until starting to soften. For a simpler sauce, skip this step.

   TRY: 2 to 4 tablespoons chopped onion, shallot, scallion, celery, pepper, carrot, or 1 clove chopped garlic.

3. **DEGLAZE** the pan with a flavorful liquid or combination of liquids: Bring to a boil, scraping the bottom of the pan to dislodge any browned bits. Boil until reduced to half the original quantity.

   TRY: ½ to 1 cup chicken or vegetable stock, red or white wine, vermouth, Madeira, or cider.

4. **THICKEN** the sauce. Add a thickening ingredient and simmer for 2 minutes. (Optional.)

   TRY: ¼ to ½ cup cream, half-and-half, or tomato puree or 1½ teaspoons tomato paste, or whisk in 1 to 2 tablespoons butter until just incorporated and remove from the heat before completely melted.

5. **SEASON** the sauce with salt, pepper, and your flavoring(s) of choice.

   TRY: chopped fresh herbs, capers, Dijon mustard, sun-dried tomatoes, or a few drops of citrus juice.

SAMPLE COMBINATIONS

French
1. Sauté the chicken.
2. Add shallot.
3. Deglaze with vermouth and chicken stock.
4. Thicken with butter.
5. Season with chopped tarragon.

Italian
1. Sauté the chicken.
2. Add garlic.
3. Deglaze with red wine.
4. Thicken with tomato puree.
5. Season with capers and chopped basil.

Southwestern
1. Sauté the chicken.
2. Add red bell pepper.
3. Deglaze with chicken stock.
4. Thicken with half-and-half.
5. Season with chopped cilantro and a little lime juice.

COMPOUND BUTTERS

Compound butters melt to make the simplest of sauces for grilled, baked, broiled, or sautéed chicken (see pages 180 to 181). Start with softened butter and stir in any of the following, or almost anything else you like; you can also use a food processor to combine. Season with salt and pepper. Use the butter immediately or make it ahead, roll it into a log, freeze it, and cut off slices as you need them to top hot chicken.

- Parsley and lemon juice
- Pine nuts, basil, and sun-dried tomatoes
- Lemon zest and crushed black peppercorns
- Soy sauce and chopped scallion
- Capers and anchovy paste
- Pecans and maple syrup
- Orange zest and cayenne pepper

- Tarragon
- Chipotle chiles, lime juice, and cilantro
- Calvados and walnuts
- Olives and crushed fennel seed
- Garlic and sage
- Red wine and roasted red pepper
- Basil and mint

CHICKEN SALADS

Don't ignore chicken salad as a basic of the quick-dinner repertoire. Serve warm or at room temperature with raw vegetables or on bread. Use leftover chicken, store-bought roasted chicken, or chicken just cooked by one of our easy Basic Cooking Methods (see pages 180 to 181) and add one of the possibilities below—or ingredients of your choice.

For creamy chicken salad, mix cooked, cut-up chicken with mayonnaise, sour cream, yogurt, or a combination of these. Season with salt and pepper to taste. If you like, add:

- Parmesan cheese and lemon juice
- Dijon mustard and dill
- Pesto and cherry tomatoes
- Watercress and cucumber
- Fennel and walnuts
- Avocado, cayenne, and lime juice
- Red onion and tarragon

For a lighter chicken salad, toss the meat with a vinaigrette made from three or four parts oil to one part vinegar and seasoned with salt and pepper. If you like, add:

- Green beans and scallions
- Bean sprouts, carrots, and sesame oil
- Bell pepper and oregano
- Artichoke hearts and lemon juice
- Radicchio and sun-dried tomatoes
- Smoked mozzarella and asparagus
- Pear and a touch of curry powder

INDEX

Page numbers in **boldface** indicate photographs 🍇 indicates wine recommendations

C